Microwave Magic
Poultry II

Grolier Limited
TORONTO

Contributors to this series:

Recipes and Technical Assistance:
École de cuisine Bachand-Bissonnette
Cooking consultants:
Denis Bissonette
Michèle Émond
Dietician:
Christiane Barbeau
Photos:
Laramée Morel Communications
Audio-Visuelles
Design:
Claudette Taillefer
Assistants:
Julie Deslauriers
Philippe O'Connor
Joan Pothier
Accessories:
Andrée Cournoyer
Writing:
Communications La Griffe Inc.
Text Consultants:
Cap et bc inc.
Advisors:
Roger Aubin
Joseph R. De Varennes
Gaston Lavoie
Kenneth H. Pearson

Assembly:
Carole Garon
Vital Lapalme
Jean-Pierre Larose
Carl Simmons
Gus Soriano
Marc Vallières
Production Managers:
Gilles Chamberland
Ernest Homewood
Production Assistants:
Martine Gingras
Catherine Gordon
Kathy Kishimoto
Peter Thomlison
Art Director:
Bernard Lamy
Editors:
Laurielle Ilacqua
Susan Marshall
Margaret Oliver
Robin Rivers
Lois Rock
Jocelyn Smyth
Donna Thomson
Dolores Williams
Development:
Le Groupe Polygone Éditeurs Inc.

We wish to thank the following firms, PIER I IMPORTS and LE CACHE POT, for their contribution to the illustration of this set.

The series editors have taken every care to ensure that the information given is accurate. However, no cookbook can guarantee the user successful results. The editors cannot accept any responsibility for the results obtained by following the recipes and recommendations given.

Canadian Cataloguing in Publication Data

Main entry under title:

Poultry II

(Microwave magic ; 7)
Translation of: La Volaille II.
Includes index.
ISBN 0-7172-2428-7

1. Cookery (Poultry).   2. Microwave cookery.
I. Series: Microwave magic (Toronto, Ont.) ; 7.

TX832.P6913 1988   641.6'65   C88-094206-1

Contents

Microwave Magic is a multi-volume set, with each volume devoted to a particular type of cooking. So, if you are looking for a chicken recipe, you simply go to one of the two volumes that deal with poultry. Each volume has its own index, and the final volume contains a general index to the complete set.

Microwave Magic puts over twelve hundred recipes at your fingertips. You will find it as useful as the microwave oven itself. Enjoy!

Note from the Editor

How to Use this Book
The books in this set have been designed to make your job as easy as possible. As a result, most of the recipes are set out in a standard way.

We suggest that you begin by consulting the information chart for the recipe you have chosen. You will find there all the information you need to decide if you are able to make it: preparation time, cost per serving, level of difficulty, number of calories per serving and other relevant details. Thus, if you have only 30 minutes in which to prepare the evening meal, you will quickly be able to tell which recipe is possible and suits your schedule.

The list of ingredients is always clearly separated from the main text. When space allows, the ingredients are shown together in a photograph so that you can make sure you have them all without rereading the list—another way of saving your valuable time. In addition, for the more complex recipes we have supplied photographs of the key stages involved either in preparation or serving.

All the dishes in this book have been cooked in a 700 watt microwave oven. If your oven has a different wattage, consult the conversion chart that appears on the following page for cooking times in different types of oven. We would like to emphasize that the cooking times given in the book are a minimum. If a dish does not seem to be cooked enough, you may return it to the oven for a few more minutes. Also, the cooking time can vary according to your ingredients: their water and fat content, thickness, shape and even where they come from. We have therefore left a blank space on each recipe page in which you can note the cooking time that suits you best. This will enable you to add a personal touch to the recipes that we suggest and to reproduce your best results every time.

Although we have put all the technical information together at the front of this book, we have inserted a number of boxed entries called **MICROTIPS** throughout to explain particular techniques. They are brief and simple, and will help you obtain successful results in your cooking.

With the very first recipe you try, you will discover just how simple microwave cooking can be and how often it depends on techniques you already use for cooking with a conventional oven. If cooking is a pleasure for you, as it is for us, it will be all the more so with a microwave oven. Now let's get on with the food.

The Editor

Key to the Symbols
For ease of reference, the following symbols have been used on the recipe information charts.

The pencil symbol is a reminder to write your cooking time in the space provided.

Level of Difficulty

Easy

Moderate

Complex

Cost per Serving

$ Inexpensive

$ $ Moderate

$ $ $ Expensive

Power Levels

All the recipes in this book have been tested in a 700 watt oven. As there are many microwave ovens on the market with different power levels, and as the names of these levels vary from one manufacturer to another, we have decided to give power levels as a percentage. To adapt the power levels given here, consult the chart opposite and the instruction manual for your oven.

Generally speaking, if you have a 500 watt or 600 watt oven you should increase cooking times by about 30% over those given, depending on the actual length of time required. The shorter the original cooking time, the greater the percentage by which it must be lengthened. The 30% figure is only an average. Consult the chart for detailed information on this topic.

Power Levels

HIGH: 100% - 90%	Vegetables (except boiled potatoes and carrots) Soup Sauce Fruits Browning ground beef Browning dish Popcorn
MEDIUM HIGH: 80% - 70%	Rapid defrosting of precooked dishes Muffins Some cakes Hot dogs
MEDIUM: 60% - 50%	Cooking tender meat Cakes Fish Seafood Eggs Reheating Boiled potatoes and carrots
MEDIUM LOW: 40%	Cooking less tender meat Simmering Melting chocolate
DEFROST: 30% **LOW: 30% - 20%**	Defrosting Simmering Cooking less tender meat
WARM: 10%	Keeping food warm Allowing yeast dough to rise

Cooking Time Conversion Chart

700 watts	600 watts*
5 s	11 s
15 s	20 s
30 s	40 s
45 s	1 min
1 min	1 min 20 s
2 min	2 min 40 s
3 min	4 min
4 min	5 min 20 s
5 min	6 min 40 s
6 min	8 min
7 min	9 min 20 s
8 min	10 min 40 s
9 min	12 min
10 min	13 min 30 s
20 min	26 min 40 s
30 min	40 min
40 min	53 min 40 s
50 min	66 min 40 s
1 h	1 h 20 min

* There is very little difference in cooking times between 500 watt ovens and 600 watt ovens.

Poultry: Everyone's Favorite

The term "poultry" refers to an impressive range of table birds, most of which are domestic fowl. For most people, however, the word is virtually synonymous with chicken, which is by far the best known and most popular of all domestic fowl. It has been a favorite since ancient times and remains so, throughout the world, today. The long and complex development of culinary traditions has led to such creations as Moroccan Couscous with Chicken, Italian Chicken Caesar, French Chicken Marengo, and Chicken American Style, to name just a few.

The immense popularity of chicken is surely due to its delicate flavor, which is a perfect foil for all kinds of accompanying ingredients: apples, bacon, ginger, cinnamon, beans, crab, grape jelly, nut stuffing, lime juice, maple syrup, oysters, pineapple, peanut butter, and many more. This versatility is a unique asset. However, other types of poultry share some of the same qualities as chicken; they, too, have been part of culinary traditions in many countries for hundreds of years and they can be prepared in a variety of different ways.

Topping the list of other types of poultry is turkey. We enjoy its delicate flavor and the many splendid ways of preparing it for festive occasions. Although poultry farmers are now responding to the demand for smaller birds, turkey still provides an economical way to feed a large gathering. The English enjoy it with red-currant jelly, whereas the Americans serve it with cranberry sauce for Thanksgiving. And to most Canadians, Christmas would simply not be Christmas without roast turkey with stuffing.

Duck and duckling are also highly regarded. It is important to distinguish between wild duck, which is usually treated as game, and domestic duck, which has fattier flesh than either turkey or chicken and is usually treated as poultry. It takes a certain amount of skill to cook duck successfully because it is not uniformly tender; however, your efforts will be rewarded by a dish with a special taste, one that is very rich.

Goose has extremely tasty meat but it is rather fatty. It is traditional fare in some European countries and has recently been gaining favor in North America. Goose reaches maturity around the Christmas holiday season, which explains why several nations regard it as their traditional Christmas dish.

Guinea fowl, which has been bred from a wild African bird, provides excellent meat. It is not nearly as well known as the types of poultry just described, but it is gaining in popularity and is being raised commercially on an ever increasing scale. It is about the size of a small chicken but has a taste similar to game, which distinguishes it from other types of poultry.

Quail, a migratory bird, is increasingly rare in the wild but is now raised commercially on a large scale. This bird can be cooked in a variety of ways to make the most of its fine flavor. Its miniature size has inspired cooks to create exotic dishes with it, ones that are often rather complex but that show it off to advantage.

There is no right or wrong occasion for serving poultry. You have therefore simply to choose the most appropriate way to satisfy your guests from the numerous recipes offered in this volume.

Simple Techniques To Make the Most of Poultry

It is necessary to know the proper techniques for defrosting and cooking any type of food in order to obtain the best results. In the last few years the microwave oven has simplified both these processes. However, you should follow a few basic principles when dealing with frozen meat so as not to spoil its flavor.

Defrosting Poultry
Many people claim that the best way to defrost any meat is to leave it in the refrigerator for several hours. However, the advanced planning required for this method is not always possible and, at such times, the microwave can be a real boon. To defrost a whole bird, place it breast side up on a rack, still in its wrapping. Divide the total defrosting time (see the chart opposite) into four periods and put the bird in the oven for the first of these periods. Then take it out of the oven and remove the wrapping. As the thinner parts—the ends of the legs, the wing tips, and the ridge of the breast along the breastbone—will defrost more quickly, shield them with aluminum foil. Put the bird back into the oven for the second defrosting period. **It is absolutely essential to allow a standing period equal to a quarter of the total oven defrosting time between each period to ensure that the heat is distributed evenly.** Halfway through the defrosting time, give the dish a half-turn and turn the bird over. Continue to alternate the periods in the microwave with standing periods. At the end of the total defrosting time, take the bird out of the oven, remove the giblets, and leave it to stand.

Defrosting Guide for Poultry
Power Level: 30%

Type of Piece	Quantity	Defrosting Time	Standing Time*
Whole chicken		8 to 12 min/kg (4 to 6 min/lb)	10 to 20 min
Quarters	4 x 225 g (8 oz)	15 min	10 min
Wings	900 g (2 lb)	15 min	10 min
	450 g (1 lb)	8 min	10 min
Drumsticks	6 x 115 g (4 oz)	12 min	10 min
Boneless Breasts	4 x 225 g (8 oz)	15 min	10 min
	2 x 225 g (8 oz)	8 min	10 min
Thighs	8 x 115 g (4 oz)	15 min	10 min
	4 x 115 g (4 oz)	8 min	10 min
Whole turkey		12 to 16 min/kg (6 to 8 min/lb)	30 to 60 min in cold water

* The time in the microwave must be alternated with standing periods equal to a quarter of the total defrosting time. So in the case of poultry, there should be four periods in the microwave, each followed by an appropriate period of standing time. The standing time in this chart refers to that time required after microwaving is complete.

Halfway through the defrosting period, give the dish a half-turn so as to ensure that the pieces defrost evenly. At the end of the process, allow the pieces to stand for ten minutes and rinse them in cold water.

Cooking Poultry

When cooking a whole bird, it is necessary to prevent overexposure of the less fleshy parts to ensure that it cooks evenly. You must therefore shield the thinner parts with aluminum foil, as in defrosting. You then place the bird on a rack, breast side up. Halfway through the cooking time (consult the chart opposite) give the dish a half-turn. (Obviously, turning the dish is not necessary if your microwave model has a built-in turntable, which ensures that the microwaves are evenly distributed throughout the meat.)

Three-quarters of the way through the cooking time turn the bird breast side down. At the end of the cooking time, pierce the thickest part of the thigh with a fork. If the juice runs clear and the flesh comes away easily, the bird is done. Let the bird stand for about ten minutes before serving to allow the heat to be evenly distributed.

Cooking Times for Poultry

Type of Piece	Quantity	Cooking Time	Standing Time
Whole chicken		22 min/kg (10 min/lb) at 70%	10 min (covered with aluminum foil)
Quarters	22 min/kg	5 min (10 min/lb) at 70%	
Wings	1 kg (2.2 lb) 450 g (1 lb)	15 to 18 min 8 min at 90%	5 min 5 min
Drumsticks	4 x 115 g (4 oz)	8 to 10 min at 70%	2 min
Cornish game hen	2	20 to 22 min/kg (9 to 10 min/lb) at 70%	10 min
Duckling		26 min/kg 12 min/lb at 70%	10 min (covered with aluminum foil
Whole turkey	29 min/kg	20 min (13 min/lb) at 70%	(covered with aluminum foil)

Adapting Recipes

There is no need to throw out all your old recipes when you purchase a microwave oven. Most of them can easily be adapted to microwave cooking. To do this successfully, you must simply bear in mind a few general principles concerning the effect of microwave energy on food.

We recommend that you begin with a recipe that you already know well. It will be much easier to work out the changes that are required if you know what the final result should be. If you are dealing with a new recipe, be sure to choose one that you are certain to like. A recipe that is not to your liking when prepared in the traditional way is unlikely to suit you better just because it has been cooked in the microwave.

To help you learn to adapt recipes to microwave cooking, consider the following two recipes for Chicken in the Pot, one prepared in the conventional way and the other, in the microwave oven. Note that boldface type is used to show the differences between the two methods.

Chicken in the Pot (Conventional Method)

Ingredients
1 chicken, 2 kg (4-1/2 lb)
3 L (about 12 cups) water
8 leeks, sliced
8 carrots, sliced diagonally
1 onion studded with
5 cloves
1 bouquet garni
pinch allspice
salt and pepper to taste
8 cabbage leaves

Stuffing:
450 g (1 lb) sausage meat, cooked
2 onions, finely chopped
2 cloves garlic, finely chopped
2 eggs, beaten
250 mL (1 cup) cubed bread (crusts removed) soaked in milk
2 sticks celery, finely chopped
30 mL (2 tablespoons) parsley, chopped

Method
— Combine all the ingredients for the stuffing and mix well.
— Stuff the chicken with a third of this mixture.
— **Put the chicken and the water in a deep dish with all the other ingredients except the cabbage leaves.**
— **Bring to the boil and simmer for 1-1/2 hours.**
— Fill the cabbage leaves with the remaining stuffing **and add them to the dish. Cook for 30 minutes.**
— **Pour off 750 mL (3 cups) of the cooking liquid and skim off the fat.** Pour into a sauceboat and serve with the bird.

Chicken in the Pot (Microwave Method)

Ingredients
1 chicken, 2 kg (4-1/2 lb)
625 mL (2-1/2 cups) water
8 leeks, sliced
8 carrots, sliced diagonally
1 onion studded with
5 cloves
1 bouquet garni
pinch allspice
salt and pepper to taste
8 cabbage leaves

Stuffing:
450 g (1 lb) sausage meat, cooked
2 onions, finely chopped
2 cloves garlic, finely chopped
2 eggs, beaten
250 mL (1 cup) cubed bread (crusts removed) soaked in milk
2 sticks celery, finely chopped
30 mL (2 tablespoons) parsley, chopped

Method
— Combine all the ingredients for the stuffing and mix well.
— Stuff the chicken with a third of this mixture.
— **Put the chicken and the water into a cooking bag and cook at 100% for 5 minutes; reduce the power to 70% and continue to cook for 15 minutes.**
— **Cook the leeks, carrots, onion and bouquet garni at 100% for 5 minutes.**
— Fill the cabbage leaves with the remaining stuffing.
— **Place the chicken, cooking stock, stuffed cabbage leaves, and the cooked vegetables in a deep dish.**
— **Season, cover, and cook at 70% for 25 minutes.**
— **Allow to stand for 10 minutes before serving.**
— Pour the cooking stock into a sauceboat and serve with the bird.

Basic Principles for Adapting Recipes

Ingredients:

Liquid ingredients slow down the cooking process in the microvave oven whereas fatty ingredients speed it up. To adapt a conventional recipe to the microwave, therefore, reduce the amount of liquid and fat to obtain the right balance. For example, in the recipe shown on this page, you might reduce the amount of water given in the conventional recipe by a third or even a half if the chicken is to be cooked the entire time in the dish. However, as the chicken is partly cooked in a cooking bag (see step 3 of the microwave recipe), which cuts down on evaporation of the stock, the amount of water in this case has been reduced by 4/5 (see the list of ingredients).

Method:
To ensure even cooking, you must give the dish or any other container a half-turn during the cooking period. It is necessary to follow the instructions given in similar recipes very precisely to ensure even cooking. In the recipe adaptation given here, this step is not necessary because the chicken is first cooked in a bag (step 3) and the second cooking period (step 7) is shorter as a result.

Cooking Times:
The microwave is a real time saver. The cooking time for poultry is half or sometimes even a third of what it is in a conventional oven. In our recipe for Chicken in the Pot, the cooking time is reduced from 2 hours to 50 minutes.

Utensils:
With the exception of containers that are metal or have a metal trim, all glassware that can be used in a conventional oven can be used in a microwave oven. Most plastic containers are also microwave safe.

Cooking Utensils

The variety of microwave dishes on the market today is so wide that you are likely to be confused about what to buy. Perhaps you have only recently acquired a microwave and are wondering if you need to buy all the special dishes manufactured for it. Relax! A few well chosen dishes will meet most of your needs. Remember that many of the dishes you already have can be safely used in the microwave, as long as they are made of glass, ceramic, porcelain (without any metal trim), or earthenware. To help you choose a good basic set of utensils, here is a description of the types most commonly used for cooking poultry in the microwave.

Rectangular Dish

This long, shallow dish is ideal for cooking a whole bird. Its low sides make it easy to manipulate the bird, which is an advantage. Because it is so large it can also be used with a rack.

Browning Dish

The browning dish has a flat base with a special coating, usually ferrite, that absorbs microwave energy as heat. It can be used to heat oil or butter for browning individual pieces or even a whole bird before you begin the cooking proper. This technique is essential if you want your bird to have a golden appearance.

MICROTIPS

To Cook Vegetables Evenly

Cooking times for vegetables vary, depending on their shape and their type. If you want to cook a variety of different vegetables together, cut those that cook more slowly into smaller pieces, all roughly the same size, and put them around the edge of the dish, where they will receive more microwave energy. Cut the vegetables that require less cooking into larger pieces and put them in the center of the dish which is penetrated by fewer microwaves. Calculate cooking times according to those that cook the most slowly and, remember to turn the dish halfway through the cooking time. When the cooking

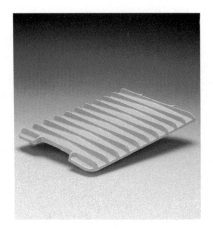 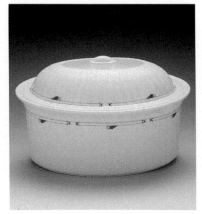 

Rack

The ridges on the rack keep the bird from sitting in its own cooking juices and therefore make for more even cooking. Liquids and fat both attract the microwaves and any parts of the bird that are left standing in the juices tend to cook more quickly than the other parts. The rack is used for the same reason when defrosting.

Deep Dish (Oval or Round)

This container holds a large volume and is used mainly to cook poultry in stock or sauce, with or without vegetables. The oval or round shape makes for more even cooking. In a dish with square corners, the food at the corners is doubly exposed to the microwaves and easily overcooks.

Bacon Rack

This dish functions as a combination baking dish and rack. However, because it is shallow it could not contain all the juice that would run out of a large bird. It is used mainly for defrosting and for cooking individual pieces. Its round shape is convenient for arranging thighs, drumsticks, and so on in the correct manner.

time is complete, test that each vegetable is done to your liking and, if necessary, cook a little longer.

Defrosting Boneless Chicken

If you wish to defrost boneless chicken, simply

put the complete package in the oven. As soon as possible, remove the wrapping and separate the pieces. Place them on a rack, taking care to have the thicker parts facing the outside of the rack, and continue the defrosting process.

How To Stuff Poultry

Allow stuffing to cool completely and fill the cavity of the bird just prior to cooking to prevent the growth of bacteria.

Planning How Much To Buy

It's one thing to cook for a large gathering and quite another to cook every day for a family. Cooking for a family is likely the more difficult task because it requires more long-term planning.

Planning means buying enough food for your needs without wasting any. It also means choosing economical cuts of meat that will not strain your budget but will provide you with the means to produce interesting and varied dishes. Good planning therefore means choosing cuts that yield a high proportion of usable food.

When you do your shopping, remember that a given weight of chicken or any other poultry may not always yield exactly the same number of portions. The amount of bone and fat (especially in the skin) can make a big difference between the weight of the bird before it is cooked and the amount of cooked meat obtained from it. The amount of lean meat after cooking varies considerably from one type of poultry to another. The size of the bird also affects the yield.

The number of portions obtained from a given weight will not be the same for a whole bird as for individual pieces. It will also vary from one type of piece to another. For example, breast portions have little bone whereas thighs contain a great deal of bone; wings are largely skin whereas a half-chicken yields a fair amount of lean meat. You must bear all these factors in mind when you buy.

Recommended Quantities for Different Types of Poultry

Type of Poultry	Quantity per serving
Whole chicken	340 g to 450 g (3/4 lb to 1 lb)
Chicken wings	appetizer: 225 g (1/2 lb) main course: 340 g to 450 g (3/4 lb to 1 lb)
Chicken thighs	1-1/2 thighs
Boneless chicken	115 g (1/4 lb)
Chicken breast	115 g (1/4 lb)
Whole duck	675 g (1-1/2 lb)
Whole goose	675 g (1-1/2 lb)
Whole guinea fowl	1/3 to 1/2 guinea fowl
Whole quail	appetizer: 1 main course: 2
Whole turkey (less than 5.4 kg (12 lb)	340 g to 450 g (3/4 lb to 1 lb)
Turkey thighs	150 g (1/3 lb)
Boneless turkey	115 g (1/4 lb)
Turkey escallops	115 g (1/4 lb)
Turkey breast	115 g (1/4 lb)

Planning Meals

Do you work to a tight schedule and find that you must forego the pleasure of browsing through cook books at your leisure? Do you find that after a hard day at work you sometimes have neither the energy nor the motivation to prepare a complicated meal and that, quite frankly, you would rather simply heat something up? If so, you should learn to take advantage of your microwave when planning meals. With a microwave, you can take an item from the freezer, defrost it, and cook it—all in the same dish. Of course, you must select the right container when preparing food for the freezer, but then you avoid the bother and the mess of transferring the food to a different container later. You also benefit from the speed with which the microwave cooks as compared with a conventional oven.

You can also prepare a large quantity of your chosen recipe, using fresh ingredients, and then freeze the cooked dish in several portions. When you want a quick and easy meal, you simply take the portions required out of the freezer and reheat them. Chicken is particularly suitable for cooking in large quantity because it is easy to prepare, either whole or in pieces, and it can be prepared in a variety of ways.

Planning Quantities

When you buy chicken or any other type of poultry, think in terms of servings rather than number of people who will be eating. By this we mean that you must take into account the appetites of the different members of your family and your guests, the way in which the meat will be prepared, the type of poultry you are using, and the amount of lean meat that you can expect to obtain from it.

Take the time to consult the chart on page 16. It will help you decide how much of a given type of poultry you should buy.

If you like to prepare meals in advance and freeze them, you can cut costs considerably by buying whole birds rather than parts. If you are cooking for several guests, recipes that call for whole birds will tend to be less expensive than recipes that use a number of the same parts.

MICROTIPS

Defrosting Chicken Pieces

To defrost chicken pieces, first remove any metal ties from the wrapped package and then put it into the microwave oven. Unwrap the chicken as soon as possible and put it on a rack. Separate the individual pieces and arrange them with the thicker parts toward the outside. Halfway through the defrosting time, give the meat a half-turn, drain it, and proceed with the defrosting. Allow the chicken to stand for 5 minutes and then wash it before cooking it. Do not forget to divide the defrosting time into four periods, with standing periods of equal length in between each.

Storing Poultry

The high cost of food makes waste unthinkable. Because we have excellent ways of storing food so that it will not spoil, there is no reason nowadays to throw food away on the grounds that it could not be used within a few days of purchase. Techniques such as refrigeration, vacuum packing, and freezing have all been perfected and are easy to use. We also know the limitations of these storage methods and how to deal with them.

For ease of reference, we are including storage tips for poultry here. Fresh poultry must be stored in the coldest part of the refrigerator or in the meat saver. It will not keep as long as cooked poultry because bacteria and toxins multiply very rapidly in uncooked meat. If you freeze fresh poultry, it will retain both its flavor and its nutritional value. However, you must take care to wrap it properly because if it is

Storage Times for Poultry

Fresh poultry	Refrigerator	Freezer
Whole chicken	1 to 2 days	6 to 7 months
Chicken pieces	1 to 2 days	4 to 5 months
Boneless chicken	1 to 2 days	6 to 7 months
Whole duck	1 to 2 days	6 to 7 months
Whole goose	1 to 2 days	3 to 4 months
Whole guinea fowl	1 to 2 days	3 months (vacuum packed)
Whole quail	1 to 2 days	3 months (vacuum packed)
Whole turkey	1 to 2 days	4 to 5 months
Turkey pieces	1 to 2 days	2 to 3 months
Boneless turkey	1 to 2 days	4 to 5 months

exposed to the cold, dry air of the freezer, it can suffer freezer burn and a general loss of quality. The packages in which you buy meat are generally not suitable for long-term storage—meaning more than a few weeks. It is better to replace them with stronger wrapping that is absolutely airtight.

Cooked poultry also freezes well and, as mentioned, keeps even longer than uncooked poultry that has been frozen. It is a good idea to freeze it as soon as possible after cooking, preferably while it is still warm, so as to retain the maximum nutritional value. Put it in containers or wrappings that exclude as much air as possible. Protect it from the cold, dry air of the freezer just as you do fresh meat. Note that whole birds, fresh or cooked, can be frozen for longer periods than individual pieces. For detailed guidelines, consult the storage times in the chart on page 18.

MICROTIPS

Cooking Individual Poultry Pieces

Pieces of poultry can be cooked quickly and evenly on a rack in a dish or on a bacon rack. First, wash and dry the pieces, and then arrange them on the rack with the thicker parts facing the outside of the dish. Use the chart on page 11 to calculate the cooking time. Give the dish a half-turn halfway through the cooking time. Let the dish stand for 2 to 5 minutes before serving, allowing the heat to be distributed evenly throughout the meat.

Leftover Poultry

Poultry leftovers can be used in a thousand and one ways. Don't throw them out; instead, store them carefully. They are bound to come in handy when you're at a loss for something to prepare.

Chilling Poultry Promptly

Cooked poultry should not be left at room temperature because bacteria will then breed rapidly. It is better to put it in the refrigerator or to freeze it while it is still warm. If you don't have time to trim the meat off the carcass, put it in the refrigerator until you do.

Freezing Poultry for Future Use

1. Chicken legs can be frozen and used later to make very tasty meals. Freeze them whole, taking care to separate them from each other with waxed paper so that you can easily take out only as many as you need for a particular occasion. You will also find it easier to defrost individual pieces when they can be separated.
2. Freeze chicken wings in the same way. They are great reheated in a spicy sauce and served with vegetables.
3. If you have leftover breast meat, freeze it separately from the dark meat, either whole or cut from the bone into large pieces. Breast meat is very tender and deserves special treatment. When you defrost it, either warm it again or reheat it in a sauce that complements the flavor and serve it with vegetables.
4. If you like hot chicken sandwiches, trim all the flesh from the carcass, cut it into small slices, and freeze it in one or two small packages so that you can defrost it quickly.
5. Drumsticks that are breaded can be frozen. Wrapped properly, they will still be crisp when they are defrosted.

A Thousand and One Ways To Serve Poultry

Are there a thousand and one ways to serve poultry? Really? We can't guarantee that this number is exact, but we do know that poultry is so popular that there are well over a hundred classic recipes. Only a few of them are outlined here to demonstrate this point.

Recipe	Method
Chicken à la king	Cooked chicken breast that is diced, sautéed in butter, and simmered in cream. To this are added green and red peppers and sautéed mushrooms. Sherry or brandy are added for flavor.
Chicken à la marseillaise	Chicken sautéed with crushed garlic, strips of green pepper, and quartered peeled tomatoes. These ingredients are sautéed in oil and the pan is deglazed with white wine and lemon juice. The final dish is garnished with parsley.
Chicken legs à l'italienne	Chicken legs filled with a chicken and mushroom stuffing, braised in an Italian sauce, and served with artichokes.
Chicken legs à la niçoise	Chicken legs filled with a chicken stuffing and braised in a mixture of white wine, thinly sliced onions, garlic, and diced tomatoes.
Duck à l'alsacienne	Individual pieces braised and served with sauerkraut cooked in white wine and potatoes. A thick brown sauce is served separately.
Duck à l'anglaise	Whole duck, braised or roasted, stuffed with sage and onion, and coated with sauce made from deglazing the pan.
Duck à la bordelaise	Roast duck, filled with a stuffing made from bread, milk, chopped liver, chopped parsley, stuffed olives, sliced sautéed mushrooms, eggs, garlic, salt, and pepper. The cooking juices are used to make a sauce that is served separately.
Goose à la danoise	Roast goose, stuffed with apples and grapes and garnished with baked apples.
Goose à la paysanne	Braised goose, garnished with thinly sliced carrots, rutabagas, celery, onions, and peas. It is served with green beans cooked in butter and mixed with a sauce that is made by skimming and thickening the stock.
Guinea fowl à l'allemande	Guinea fowl larded with bacon, braised, and served on a bed of sauerkraut mixed with poached oysters. Served with a Madeira sauce.
Guinea fowl casserole	Guinea fowl roasted in a deep dish of porcelain or glass and served from the casserole with a sauce.
Turkey with almonds	Roast turkey, served with its own cooking juices, filled with a stuffing made from butter, eggs, breadcrumbs, ground almonds, salt, and nutmeg.
Turkey gourmet style	Roast turkey, stuffed with chestnuts and cooked with little sausages. The pan is deglazed to make a sauce.
Turkey supreme à la mode du chef	Supremes of young turkey, poached until tender with oysters and stuffed olives in stock and served with a sauce made from the stock. This dish is garnished with julienned strips of red pepper.

Vegetables To Serve with Poultry

As everyone knows, vegetables are an important part of any diet and are normally served with poultry as with any other meat.

Vegetables can be used merely as a decorative garnish—strips of pepper, tomatoes, parsley and many other vegetables that can be eaten raw are frequently used for this purpose. Some recipes, however, suggest that you cook these same vegetables with the bird. The aim here is to achieve a subtle blend of flavors rather than mere eye appeal. When you do want to braise or poach a bird with a number of vegetables, select the so-called aromatic vegetables, ones that will impart their distinctive taste to the meat during cooking. It is not necessary to choose exotic vegetables; carrots, rutabagas, onions, garlic, and celery are the most commonly used aromatic vegetables. If you prefer, the vegetables can be cooked separately, steamed or braised, in order to make the most of the distinctive flavor of each. These vegetables are served with the meat, usually with a knob of butter or coated in a sauce made from the cooking juices of the bird.

There are countless vegetables that are suitable for serving with poultry, many of them going well together. Among the most popular are peas, snow peas, and broad beans; leeks, green onions, and onions; rutabagas, potatoes, and carrots. Other popular choices include celery, artichokes, eggplant, squash, peppers, sautéed cucumber, mushrooms, and okra.

If you want to serve several accompanying vegetables and cook them at the same time, be sure to choose those that require roughly the same cooking time, or the faster cooking vegetables will be overdone. If, however, you want to serve both quick and slow cooking vegetables, either cook them separately or add those that cook faster partway through the cooking time.

Turkey with Cornbread Stuffing

Level of Difficulty	🍴
Preparation Time	20 min
Cost per Serving	$ $
Number of Servings	16
Nutritional Value	445 calories 61.7 g protein 4.9 g lipids
Food Exchanges	5 oz meat 1 fat exchange 1 vegetable exchange
Cooking Time	29 min/kg (13 min/lb) + 6 min
Standing Time	10 min
Power Level	100%, 70%
Write Your Cooking Time Here	

Ingredients
1 turkey, 4.5 kg (10 lb)
cleaned, rinsed, and dried
125 mL (1/2 cup) onion,
diced
125 mL (1/2 cup) celery,
diced
30 mL (2 tablespoons) butter
500 mL (2 cups) mushrooms,
diced
250 mL (1 cup) hot chicken
stock
500 mL (2 cups) cornbread
crumbs
50 mL (1/4 cup) chicken
concentrate
paprika to taste

Method
— Put the onion, celery, and
  butter in a dish; cover and
  cook at 100% for 3 to 4
  minutes.
— Add the mushrooms,
  cover, and cook at 100%
  for 2 minutes.
— Add the hot chicken stock
  and mix well, stir in the
  crumbs, and stuff the
  turkey.
— Truss the turkey.
— Combine the paprika and
  chicken concentrate and
  sprinkle over the turkey.
— Cover and cook, breast
  side up, at 70% for half
  the total time, allowing 29
  min/kg (13 min/lb).
— Turn the turkey over,
  cover again, and continue
  to cook.
— Allow to stand for 10
  minutes and serve with the
  stuffing.

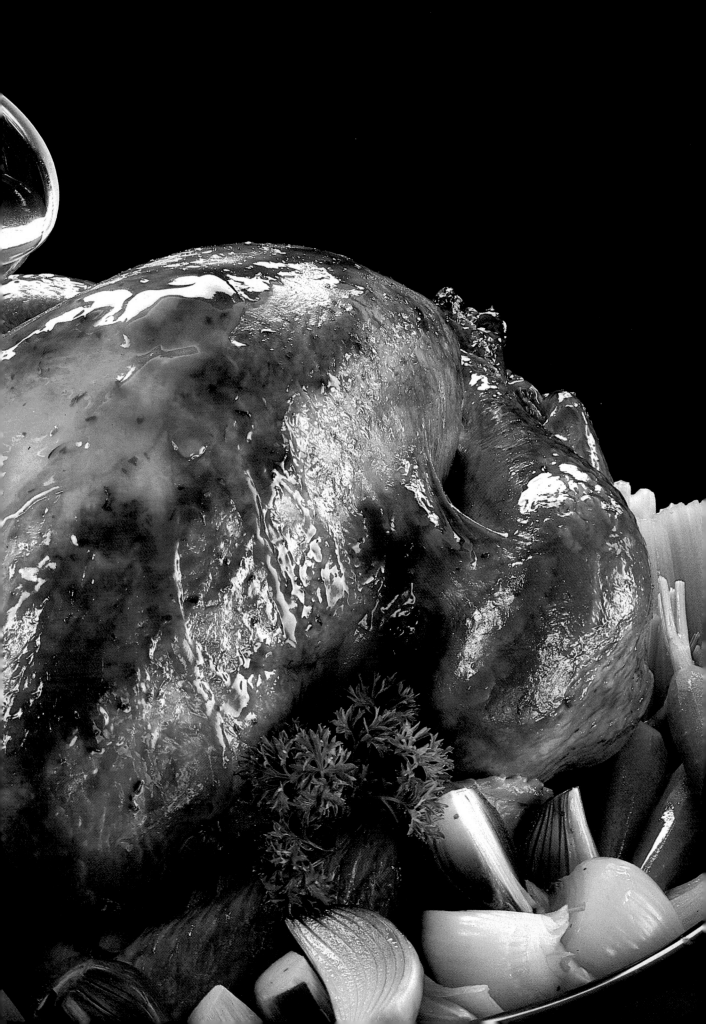

Turkey with Vegetables

Level of Difficulty	🍴
Preparation Time	20 min
Cost per Serving	$
Number of Servings	6
Nutritional Value	406 calories 37.9 g protein 16.5 g lipids
Food Exchanges	4 oz meat 2 fat exchanges 3 vegetable exchanges
Cooking Time	37 min
Standing Time	5 min
Power Level	100%, 70%
Write Your Cooking Time Here	

Ingredients

1.3 kg (3 lb) turkey, boned, skinned, and cubed
60 mL (4 tablespoons) butter
60 mL (4 tablespoons) flour
500 mL (2 cups) chicken stock
7 mL (1/2 tablespoon) poultry seasoning
250 mL (1 cup) onion, sliced
250 mL (1 cup) celery, diced
250 mL (1 cup) carrot, sliced
250 mL (1 cup) potato, diced
75 mL (1/3 cup) water
340 g (12 oz) frozen peas
salt and pepper to taste

Method

— Preheat a browning dish at 100% for 7 minutes; meanwhile, cut the vegetables and set them aside.
— Put the butter in the heated dish and heat at 100% for 30 seconds.
— Brown the cubes of turkey in the dish.
— Dredge the turkey cubes with flour, stir in the chicken stock, and add the poultry seasoning.
— Cook at 100% for 4 to 5 minutes, or until the mixture thickens. Stir halfway through the cooking time.

Turkey with Vegetables

Assemble all the ingredients for this simple and economical recipe for turkey with vegetables.

Brown the turkey cubes and then dredge them with flour.

Add the chicken stock and proceed to cook as directed in the recipe.

— Put the onion, celery, carrot and potato in another dish and add the water. Cover and cook at 100% minutes, stirring after 4 minutes.

— Combine the vegetables and their cooking liquid with the turkey; cover and cook at 70% for 10 minutes.
— Stir well, add the frozen peas, and season.

— Cover and cook at 70% for 10 to 15 minutes, or until the turkey is tender, stirring halfway through the cooking time.
— Allow to stand for 5 minutes before serving.

MICROTIPS

How To Use Cooking Bags

Cooking bags are very useful if you want to poach a whole bird in the microwave. However, the following safety measures should be observed when using them:

1. Never use a metal tie to close a cooking bag for the microwave. It could cause arcing and seriously damage your

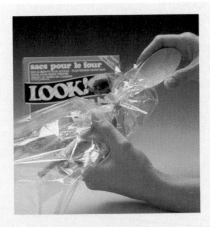

oven. Plastic ties that are perfectly safe for microwave use are available.

2. If you do not have

plastic ties, cut a narrow strip off the bag and use it to tie the bag shut. If, however, you plan to use cooking bags frequently, be sure to have a supply of ties on hand.

3. To allow the steam to escape during cooking, do not fasten the bag too securely. To be sure of this, wrap the neck of the bag around the handle of a wooden spoon, twist the tie around the bag and handle together, and then remove the spoon.

Sauces

The word "sauce" comes from the Latin *salsus,* meaning "salted." An explanation for this probably lies in the fact that salt has long been the basic condiment for seasoning food, but not all sauces are salted. Sauces vary in consistency from thin and liquid to thick and creamy. They are usually made from aromatic ingredients with a certain fat content and may be served as an accompaniment to food or may be cooked with it. Sauces should always complement the dish they accompany.

Sauces were once an indicator of prosperity. In the past, people tended to prepare food without sauces when times were hard, and they developed an impressive repertoire of sauces when times were prosperous.

A number of civilizations have developed their culinary traditions to a high level of sophistication. In the Far East, the Middle East and North Africa, for example, people have been perfecting their traditional dishes for centuries. These civilizations have naturally developed a wide range of sauces.

Most of the sauces made to go with poultry are prepared from the cooking liquid. They may be made by deglazing the pan in which the bird is roasted or, if the bird is poached or braised, from the liquid in which it is cooked. These two basic approaches have given rise to a multitude of variations, and you should choose one to suit whatever recipe you are using. For example, the supreme, or the breast meat, has a delightful texture and delicate flavor; it goes best with a light tasting velouté sauce. A hint of spiciness in the sauce gives the dish a distinctive character. By contrast, some of the less tender chicken pieces are better cooked in or served with a highly spiced sauce. A barbecue or chili sauce goes very well with chicken wings or thighs. On the other hand, poultry having a very pronounced flavor, such as duck, benefits from being served with sauces made from rather acidic fruit: cherries, apples, or oranges. Some combinations of poultry and particular sauces are so successful that they have become classics.

Always pay special attention to the kind of sauce that you are choosing to serve with poultry. Showing this touch of refinement on festive occasions as well as for everyday meals will enable you to produce countless variations in cooking with poultry. Your guests and your family need never become tired of the same old meat.

Marinated Turkey Cutlets

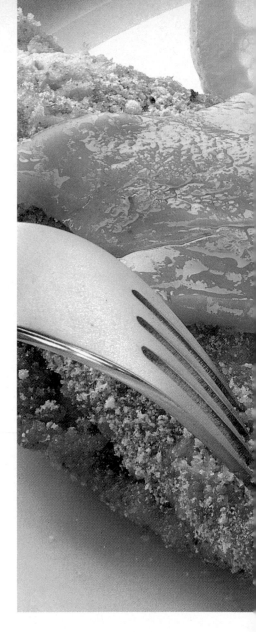

Level of Difficulty	🍴
Preparation Time	10 min*
Cost per Serving	$ $
Number of Servings	4
Nutritional Value	524 calories 30.8 g protein 29.7 g lipids
Food Exchanges	4 oz meat 3 fat exchanges 1 bread exchange
Cooking Time	9 min
Standing Time	2 min
Power Level	70%
Write Your Cooking Time Here	

* The cutlets should be left to marinate for 1 to 2 hours.

Ingredients
4 turkey cutlets, 60 to 85 g (2 to 3 oz) each, 6 mm (1/4 inch) thick
75 mL (1/3 cup) mayonnaise
75 mL (1/3 cup) sour cream
15 mL (1 tablespoon) Dijon mustard
2 mL (1/2 teaspoon) Worcestershire sauce
pinch cayenne pepper
500 mL (2 cups) onion-flavored croutons, crushed
4 slices cheddar cheese, cut into strips

Method
— In a bowl, combine the mayonnaise, sour cream, mustard, Worcestershire sauce and cayenne pepper. Mix well.
— Place the cutlets in this mixture and allow to marinate for 1 to 2 hours.
— After marinating, wipe the excess marinade off the cutlets and coat them with the croûton crumbs.
— Place the cutlets on a rack, leave uncovered, and cook at 70% for 3 minutes.
— Turn the cutlets over, garnish with the strips of cheese, and continue to cook at 70% for another 3 minutes.
— Give the rack a half-turn and cook at 70% for 2 to 3 minutes, or until the cutlets are tender.
— Allow to stand for 2 minutes before serving.

Make the marinade as described and marinate the cutlets. This flavoring is bound to please your guests.

Remove the cutlets from the marinade, wipe off the excess, and coat with the crumbs. This coating will give the cutlets an attractive golden appearance.

After the first cooking period, turn the cutlets over and garnish them with the strips of cheese.

Turkey Sandwich

Level of Difficulty	🍴
Preparation Time	5 min
Cost per Serving	$
Number of Servings	2
Nutritional Value	621 calories 45 g protein 32.4 g lipids
Food Exchanges	5 oz meat 3 fat exchanges 2 bread exchanges
Cooking Time	1 min
Standing Time	None
Power Level	90%
Write Your Cooking Time Here	

Ingredients
225 g (1/2 lb) cooked turkey, chopped
45 mL (3 tablespoons) mayonnaise
15 mL (1 tablespoon) Dijon mustard
5 mL (1 teaspoon) relish
2 hamburger buns, toasted and cut in half
2 slices Gruyère cheese
2 slices tomato

Method
— Combine the turkey, mayonnaise, mustard, and relish in a bowl and mix.
— Spread this mixture on the bottom half of each bun.
— Place a slice of Gruyère cheese and a slice of tomato on each of the other halves of the buns.
— Heat the bun halves in the microwave at 90% for 45 to 60 seconds.
— Put the top half of each bun on the lower half and serve immediately.

Assemble all the ingredients for this simple recipe—one that is just perfect when you feel a sudden pang of hunger.

MICROTIPS

How To Roast Poultry Successfully

It is a good idea to truss poultry before you cook it. Trussing ensures that the bird will keep its shape and will therefore look more attractive when you serve it. As poultry should not be allowed to cook in its own juices, place it on a

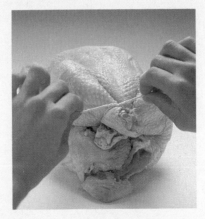

rack or, if you do not have one, on an upside down saucer. If you do use a saucer, the problem of how to break the suction can be avoided by slipping a toothpick under one edge. To enhance the flavor of chicken or turkey, baste it with a suitable liquid. If possible, use sweet, unsalted butter for basting to prevent the skin from cracking or going hard during cooking.

Goose: Traditional and Delicious

Along with the duck, hen and rooster, the goose conjures up two distinct images; one is of fairy tales and legends in which the goose takes on its own special persona, and the other is of large tables groaning under the weight of festive fare, upon which the goose makes a magnificent centerpiece. Let us focus on this second image.

Goose has played a large role in cooking traditions for a very long time. In fact, some archaeologists claim that the goose was a domestic bird in Neolithic times, and other information suggests that it was raised as domestic fowl nearly 3500 years ago in the region that forms present-day Germany.

Historians believe that it was the Greeks who introduced the Romans to the culinary delights of the goose. Once conquered by the Romans, they taught their overlords how to fatten goose for the table.

Although goose has long been highly prized in many countries, it was not until more recent times that it gained popularity in North America. Some countries in central Europe and Scandinavia have long made it their choice for the traditional Christmas feast, but well into the nineteenth century many North American connoisseurs of fine food still considered it a poor substitute for chicken. Today, however, goose is extremely popular both for those very special meals such as Christmas dinner and for more ordinary occasions.

It is important to distinguish between wild goose and domestic goose. The former has lean meat because it uses so much energy in flying. The latter has much fattier meat, which is more tender and has a more subtle flavor. Domestic goose is by far the most popular choice between the two.

A domestic goose lays 5 or 6 eggs in the spring. The young goslings take 7 to 8 months to reach their ideal weight for the table, which is between 2.75 and 3.5 kg (6 and 8 lbs). Although turkey vies with goose in popularity, goose has some undisputed advantages, chief among which is the number of ways in which it can be prepared.

Goose with Pears in Brandy

Level of Difficulty	🍴
Preparation Time	20 min
Cost per Serving	$ $
Number of Servings	6
Nutritional Value	535 calories 49.1 g protein 21.3 g lipids
Food Exchanges	5 oz meat 1 fat exchange 1 vegetable exchange 1-1/2 fruit exchanges
Cooking Time	35 min/kg (16 min/lb) + 9 min
Standing Time	10 min
Power Level	70%, 90%
Write Your Cooking Time Here	

Ingredients
1 goose, 3 to 4 kg (7 to 9 lb)
1 large onion, cut in half
1 carrot, cut into sticks
45 mL (3 tablespoons)
chicken stock
15 mL (1 tablespoon) paprika
6 pears, cut in half
1 lemon, cut in half
30 mL (2 tablespoons)
brandy

Method
— Prick the goose in several
  places with a fork.
— Place the onion halves and
  carrot sticks inside the
  body cavity.
— Combine the chicken
  stock and paprika and
  baste the goose with this
  liquid.
— Place the goose on a rack,
  leave uncovered, and cook
  at 70%, allowing 35
  min/kg (16 min/lb), or
  until the meat is tender.
— When the bird is done,
  take it out of the oven
  and set aside 60 mL (4

tablespoons) of the
cooking juice; cover the
bird with aluminum foil,
putting the shiny side next
to the flesh. Let stand for
10 minutes.
— Arrange the pears in a
  dish and sprinkle them
  with the reserved cooking
  juices and the juice from
  the lemon.
— Cover the pears and cook
  them at 90% for 5 to 6
  minutes, or until they are
  soft.

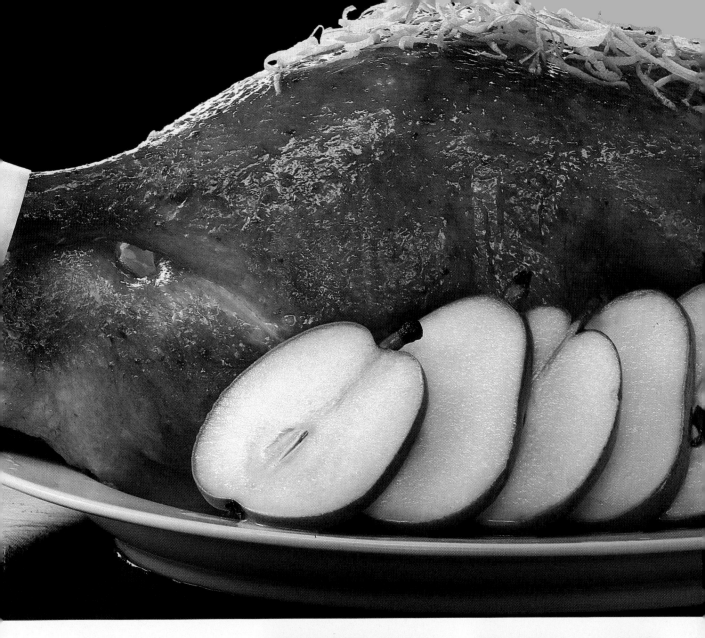

— Sprinkle the pears with the brandy.
— After removing the aluminum foil, place the goose on a serving platter, and deglaze the pan.
— Remove the cooking juice from the pears, mix it with the meat juice, and heat at 90% for 2 to 3 minutes, stirring once.
— Arrange the pears around the goose and sprinkle with the heated cooking juices.

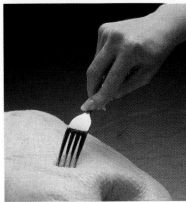

Prick the goose with a fork in several places.

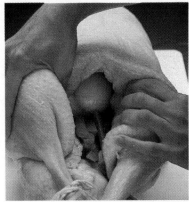

Put the onion halves and carrot sticks into the body cavity and then close the opening.

Goose French Style

Level of Difficulty	(utensils icon)
Preparation Time	10 min
Cost per Serving	$ $
Number of Servings	6
Nutritional Value	510 calories 51.9 g protein 38.5 g lipids
Food Exchanges	5 oz meat 1-1/2 fat exchanges 3 vegetable exchanges
Cooking Time	22 min/kg (10 min/lb)
Standing Time	5 min
Power Level	100%, 70%
Write Your Cooking Time Here	(apple and pencil icon)

Ingredients
1 goose, 3 kg (7 lb), cut into serving pieces
45 mL (3 tablespoons) oil
lettuce leaves
pepper to taste
340 g (12 oz) frozen peas

Method
— Preheat a browning dish at 100% for 7 minutes.
— Pour the oil into the hot dish and return it to the oven at 100% for 30 seconds.
— Brown the pieces of goose in the oil and prick them in several places with a fork.
— Arrange the lettuce leaves in the bottom of a dish, place the goose on top, and season with pepper.
— Cover the dish and cook at 70% until the meat is tender, allowing 22 min/kg (10 min/lb). Give the dish a half-turn halfway through the cooking time.
— Add the frozen peas 30 minutes before the end of the cooking time.
— Allow to stand for 5 minutes before serving.

Assemble the ingredients for this French-style goose recipe. Goose is rapidly gaining popularity in North America.

Use a fork to prick each piece of goose in several places to allow the cooking juices to escape.

Arrange the goose pieces on a bed of lettuce, cover, and place in the oven.

Stuffing: A Culinary Success

The "oohs" and "aahs" that are usually heard when roast turkey is brought to the Christmas table are for the bird itself and not for the stuffing. However, if the turkey were found not to contain stuffing, you would certainly hear cries of disappointment.

Stuffing is a mixture of raw or cooked ingredients that are chopped, mixed together and seasoned. It is used as a filling for game (pheasant, for example), some vegetables (peppers), eggs, pasta (cannelloni), fish (pike), meat (suckling pig) and all types of poultry. Stuffing has other uses too. It is the basis of many pâtés, terrines, galantines and sausages. It is also used in hot canapés, as a filling for pies, and in other similar ways.

There are two main categories of stuffing: lean and fatty. However, even lean stuffings need a certain amount of fat (such as cream) to give them the required "softness" in texture.

Stuffing for poultry is usually made from finely ground meat. The giblets, such as the livers and hearts, are frequently used, but the dark meat of poultry can also used in stuffing. Other ingredients are then added: whole eggs or the yolks or whites alone, mushrooms, onions, bread soaked in milk, ham, foie gras, and so on. Finally, appropriate herbs and spices are added to give the stuffing its distinctive flavor.

This mixture is already very rich but, for extra sophistication, you can add certain types of alcohol, dried fruits such as prunes and raisins, or such nuts as almonds.

There are countless recipes for stuffing, and it would be impossible to present them all here. However, it is worth emphasizing that a stuffing that goes very well with one type of poultry may not suit another at all. Consider the following examples. In Scandinavian tradition and in that of several countries in central Europe, the Christmas goose is served with a stuffing of fruit (apples, plums) or vegetables (potatoes, cabbage). The latter provides a pleasant contrast with the richness of the goose and is very nutritious. In our tradition, however, the Christmas turkey is stuffed with bread soaked in milk. This basic mixture can be seasoned and flavored in a variety of ways—raisins, for instance, are a popular ingredient. The distinctive flavor of duck is complemented by a simple vegetable-based stuffing, using, perhaps, chard or spinach. The addition of a soft white cheese gives this type of stuffing a lovely creamy texture. These few examples should give you an idea of the range of possibilities for stuffings to use with poultry.

The following two pages offer six different recipes for stuffing that we think are among the most interesting. Use them as a change from your usual recipes—your guests will be delighted.

Suggested Stuffings for Poultry

Liver Stuffing for Turkey

Ingredients

1 onion, finely chopped
115 g (4 oz) ground pork, cooked
115 g (4 oz) cooked turkey liver, coarsely ground
1/2 clove garlic
fine herbs (thyme, sage, basil and parsley) to taste
250 mL (1 cup) bread cubes (crusts removed) soaked in milk
2 egg yolks
50 mL (1/4 cup) chicken stock

Method
— Put the onion in a dish, cover, and cook at 100% for 2 to 3 minutes.
— Combine the ground pork and turkey liver.
— Mix the garlic, fine herbs, and bread soaked in milk with the cooked onion and the meat and put the mixture through a grinder.
— In another dish, mix the egg yolks with the chicken stock.
— Stir the liquid into the meat mixture and mix well together before stuffing the bird.

Potato Stuffing

Ingredients

30 mL (2 tablespoons) oil
1 clove garlic, chopped
1 large onion, finely chopped
1 stick celery, finely chopped
225 g (8 oz) chicken liver, ground
400 mL (1-2/3 cups) mashed potato to which you have added 5 mL (1 teaspoon) baking powder
250 mL (1 cup) croutons
60 mL (4 tablespoons) parsley, chopped
15 mL (1 tablespoon) salt
5 mL (1 teaspoon) thyme
2 mL (1/2 teaspoon) pepper
2 mL (1/2 teaspoon) Tabasco sauce

Method
— Heat the oil in a dish at 100% for 30 seconds.
— Put the garlic, onion, and celery in the dish and cook at 100% for 2 to 3 minutes.
— Add the chicken liver and cook at 90% for 2 to 3 minutes.
— Add the remaining ingredients and mix well.
— Stuff the bird with this mixture.

Mushroom Stuffing

Ingredients

15 mL (1 tablespoon) butter
125 mL (1/2 cup) mushrooms, thinly sliced
1 onion, finely chopped
115 g (4 oz) liver pâté
125 mL (1/2 cup) stale bread, crusts removed
30 mL (2 tablespoons) beaten egg
salt and pepper to taste

Method
— Melt the butter in a dish at 100% for 30 seconds.
— Put the mushrooms and onion in the dish, cover, and cook at 100% for 2 to 3 minutes.
— Take the cooked mushrooms and onions out of the oven, add the remaining ingredients, and mix well before stuffing the bird.

Apple Stuffing

Ingredients
6 slices bacon, diced
30 mL (2 tablespoons) margarine
500 mL (2 cups) apple, diced
45 mL (3 tablespoons) onion, thinly sliced
50 mL (1/4 cup) celery leaves, chopped
15 mL (1 tablespoon) parsley, chopped
7 mL (1/2 tablespoon) salt
5 mL (1 teaspoon) sage
5 mL (1 teaspoon) savory
5 mL (1 teaspoon) thyme or marjoram
1 L (4 cups) cubed bread, crusts removed

Method
— Cook the bacon on a rack at 100% for 3 to 4 minutes and set aside.
— Melt the margarine in a dish at 100% for 40 seconds.
— Add the apples, onion, and celery leaves and cook at 100% for 2 to 3 minutes.
— Add the remaining ingredients as well as the bacon and mix well.
— (Yields approximately 1 L (4 cups) stuffing.)

Cranberry Stuffing

Ingredients
75 mL (1/3 cup) butter
1 L (4 cups) breadcrumbs
250 mL (1 cup) cranberries, chopped
50 mL (1/4 cup) sugar
pinch cinnamon
125 mL (1/2 cup) orange juice

Method
— Heat the butter in a dish at 100% for 1 minute.
— Add the breadcrumbs to the melted butter and mix well.
— Add the cranberries, sugar, and cinnamon and mix well.
— Pour the orange juice into the mixture slowly, stirring well, until it forms a compact ball.
— Stuff the bird with this mixture.

Oyster Stuffing

Ingredients
225 g (8 oz) bacon fat
75 mL (1/3 cup) onion, finely chopped
175 mL (3/4 cup) celery, finely chopped
625 mL (2-1/2 cups) oysters, chopped or ground
liquid form the oysters
50 mL (1/4 cup) butter
50 mL (1/4 cup) parsley, chopped
2 L (8 cups) bread (crusts removed), diced and toasted
15 mL (1 tablespoon) savory
salt and pepper to taste

Method
— Put the bacon fat in a dish with the onion and celery and cook at 100% for 4 to 5 minutes.
— Add the oysters, reserving the liquid, and cook at 100% for 2 minutes.
— Stir in the oyster liquid, butter, and parsley; cover and refrigerate until cool.
— Add the remaining ingredients to the cooked mixture and mix well.

Coq au Vin

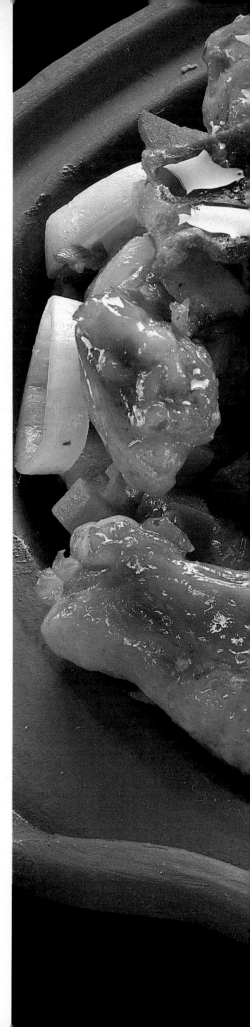

Level of Difficulty	░░ ░░
Preparation Time	40 min
Cost per Serving	$ $
Number of Servings	8
Nutritional Value	544 calories 58.6 g protein 22 g lipids
Food Exchanges	4 oz meat 2 fat exchanges 3 vegetable exchanges 1 bread exchange
Cooking Time	18 to 22 min/kg (7 to 10 min/lb) + 27 min
Standing Time	None
Power Level	100%, 90%, 70%, 50%
Write Your Cooking Time Here	

Ingredients

1 chicken, 2.7 kg (6 lb), cut into serving pieces
45 mL (3 tablespoons) oil
4 slices bacon, cut into four
3 onions, sliced
3 carrots, cut into small cubes
30 mL (2 tablespoons) flour
salt and pepper to taste
60 mL (4 tablespoons) brandy
125 mL (1/2 cup) dry white wine
1 bouquet garni
500 mL (2 cups) button mushrooms
6 slices bread, toasted, crusts removed, and cut into triangles
30 mL (2 tablespoons) parsley, chopped

Method

— Preheat a browning dish at 100% for 7 minutes.
— Pour the oil into the preheated dish and heat in the oven at 100% for 30 seconds.
— Remove the dish from the oven, brown the chicken pieces, and transfer them to another dish.
— Put the bacon in the browning dish, leave uncovered, and cook at 100% for 4 to 5 minutes; remove the bacon and set aside.
— Put the onions and carrots in the same dish. Cover and cook at 100% for 5 to 7 minutes, stirring after 3 minutes.

⟹

Coq au vin

Assemble all the ingredients for this tasty dish, one that will bring you rounds of applause.

Sear the chicken pieces in the browning dish to give them an attractive golden appearance.

Dredge the vegetables lightly with flour so that the cooking juices will thicken.

— Add the flour to the vegetables, mix well, and season with salt and pepper.

— Arrange the chicken pieces on the vegetable mixture, sprinkle with the brandy, and flambé.

— When the flames die down add the wine, cover, and cook at 90% for 2 minutes, or until the liquid boils.

— Remove the chicken pieces, put in a deep dish, and set the vegetables aside.

— Using a wooden spoon, scrape the bottom of the original dish to remove the cooking particles, mix with the juices, and pour over the chicken pieces. If there is not enough liquid to cover the chicken, add more white wine.

— Add the bouquet garni to the chicken dish, cover and cook at 70% for 18 to 22 min/kg (7 to 10 min/lb), or until the meat is tender. Give the dish a half-turn halfway through the cooking time. Remove the chicken pieces and set aside.

— Put the mushrooms in another dish, cover, and cook at 100% for 2 to 3 minutes. Set aside.

— Strain the liquid in which the chicken was cooked through a very fine sieve, pushing it through with a pestle.

— Skim the resulting sauce of as much fat as possible.

— If the sauce is too thin, thicken it with a little cornstarch dissolved in cold water.

— Put the chicken pieces, vegetables, mushrooms, and bacon in the deep dish. Add the sauce, cover, and cook at 50% for 8 to 10 minutes. Give the dish a half-turn halfway through the cooking time.

— When the cooking is complete, arrange the chicken pieces in a large serving dish and surround them with the vegetables and bacon.

— Dip the tips of the toasted triangles in the sauce and then in the parsley. Arrange them around the chicken with the tips pointing outward.

— Pour the sauce over the chicken and sprinkle with parsley.

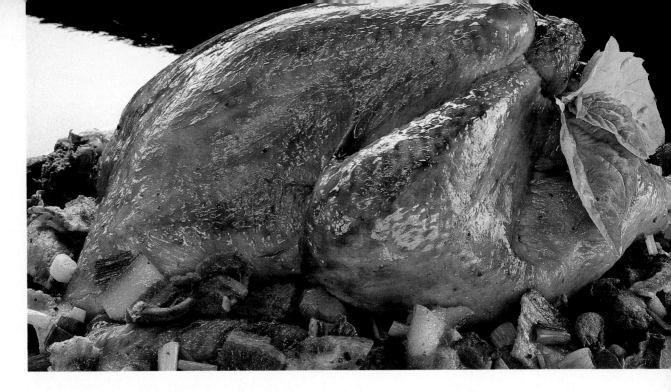

Stuffed Roast Chicken

Ingredients
1 chicken, 2.7 kg (6 lb)
45 mL (3 tablespoons) oil
4 slices bacon
225 g (8 oz) chicken liver,

coarsely ground
50 mL (1/4 cup) green onion,
chopped
salt and pepper to taste
poultry seasoning to taste

Level of Difficulty	🍴
Preparation Time	10 min
Cost per Serving	$ $
Number of Servings	8
Nutritional Value	478 calories 63 g protein 22.4 g lipids
Food Exchanges	5 oz meat 2 fat exchanges
Cooking Time	22 min/kg (10 min/lb) + 8 min
Standing Time	4 min
Power Level	100%, 70%
Write Your Cooking Time Here	

Method
— Preheat a browning dish at 100% for 7 minutes.
— Pour the oil into the preheated dish and heat at 100% for 30 seconds.
— Brown the chicken breast in the hot oil until the skin is an attractive golden color and set aside.
— Cut the bacon into small pieces, put them in the browning dish, and cook at 100% for 3 to 4 minutes.
— Add the chicken liver to the bacon and cook at 100% for 3 to 4 minutes, stirring halfway through the cooking time.
— Add the green onion, salt, pepper, and seasoning and mix well.
— Stuff the bird with this mixture.
— Put the chicken on a rack, leave uncovered, and cook at 70%, allowing 22 min/kg (10 min/lb).
— Allow to stand for 4 minutes before serving.

Duck Provençale

Level of Difficulty	
Preparation Time	10 min
Cost per Serving	$ $
Number of Servings	6
Nutritional Value	304 calories 33.5 g protein 14.6 g lipids
Food Exchanges	4.5 oz meat 2 vegetable exchanges
Cooking Time	33 min/kg (15 min/lb) + 5 min
Standing Time	5 min
Power Level	100%, 70%
Write Your Cooking Time Here	

Ingredients
1 duck, approximately 2 kg (4-1/2 lb), cut into serving pieces
1 796 mL (28 oz) can tomatoes, crushed
2 cloves garlic, crushed
3 anchovy fillets, cut into pieces
20 black olives, cut in half

Method
— Put the pieces of duck in a deep dish with the thicker parts facing the outer edge.
— Combine all the other ingredients in another dish, mix, and heat at 100% for 4 to 5 minutes.
— Pour the hot tomato mixture over the duck.
— Cover the dish and cook at 70%, allowing 33 min/kg (15 min/lb).
— Rearrange the pieces of duck at least twice during the cooking period.
— Allow to stand for 5 minutes before serving.

Assemble all the ingredients for this fragrant dish, which is reminiscent of the French region of Provence.

Place the duck in a deep dish with the thicker parts facing the outer edge.

Pour the hot tomato mixture over the duck, cover and cook as directed in the recipe.

Rearrange the pieces of duck at least twice during the cooking time.

Roast Duck in Sauce Piquante

Level of Difficulty	
Preparation Time	15 min
Cost per Serving	$ $ $
Number of Servings	6
Nutritional Value	412 calories 36.3 g protein 18 g lipids
Food Exchanges	4 oz meat 1 fat exchange 2 vegetable exchanges 1 fruit exchange
Cooking Time	26 min/kg (12 min/lb) + 13 min
Standing Time	10 min
Power Level	70%, 100%
Write Your Cooking Time Here	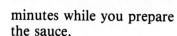

Ingredients
1 duck, 2 to 2.5 kg (4-1/2 to 5-1/2 lb)
pepper to taste
2 mL (1/2 teaspoon) rosemary
1 carrot, coarsely chopped
1 onion, chopped
1 tomato, cored and cut into small pieces
250 mL (1 cup) chicken stock
45 mL (3 tablespoons) sugar
75 mL (1/3 cup) butter
30 mL (2 tablespoons) cider vinegar
250 mL (1 cup) red berries of your choice, stewed
45 mL (3 tablespoons) brandy
2 mL (1/2 teaspoon) ginger

Method
— Wash the duck thoroughly and trim off excess fat.
— Season the inside and outside of the duck with pepper and sprinkle the inside with rosemary.
— Place the duck, breast side down, on a rack and cook at 70%, allowing 26 min/kg (12 min/lb).
— When the cooking period is over, remove the bird and cover it with aluminum foil, putting the shiny side next to the flesh. Let stand for 10 minutes while you prepare the sauce.
— Put the carrots in another dish, cover, and cook at 100% for 4 to 5 minutes, stirring halfway through the cooking time.
— Add the onion and tomato, cover, and cook at 100% for 3 to 4 minutes, or until the carrots are soft. Set aside.
— Remove as much fat as possible from the duck pan; deglaze the pan with the chicken stock, strain the resulting juice through

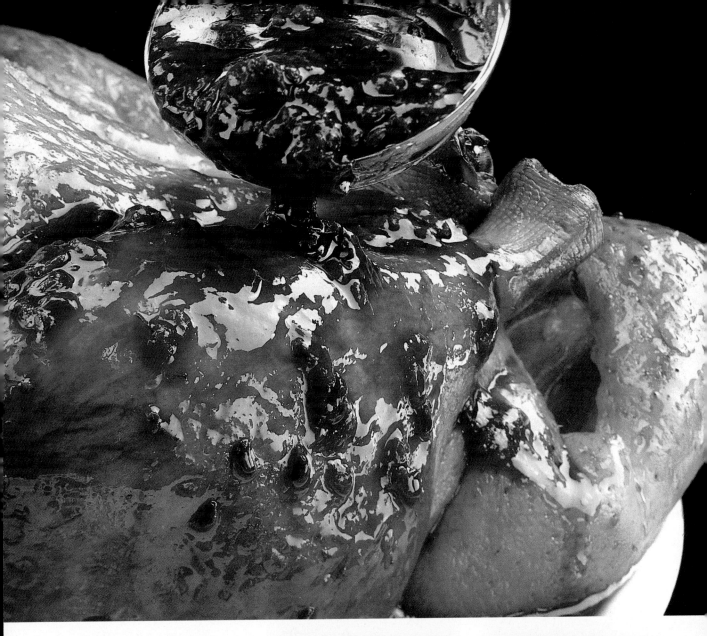

a sieve, and set aside.
— Mix the sugar with the
  butter and heat at 100%,
  until the mixture begins to
  turn brown.
— Combine this mixture with
  the vinegar, berries,
  brandy and ginger and stir
  well.
— Add the vegetables and
  the strained cooking juices
  and cook at 100% for 3 to
  4 minutes, stirring halfway
  through the cooking time.
— Cut the duck into serving
  pieces and coat with the
  sauce.

*Assemble all the ingredients
for this dish, which looks as
good as it tastes.*

*Deglaze the duck pan with the
chicken stock and strain to
remove some of the fat. Set
aside to combine with the
berry mixture.*

Oriental Duck

Level of Difficulty	🍴🍴
Preparation Time	15 min*
Cost per Serving	$ $ $
Number of Servings	4
Nutritional Value	370 calories 36.6 g protein 17.2 g lipids
Food Exchanges	4 oz meat 1 fat exchange
Cooking Time	26 min/kg (12 min/lb) + 4 min
Standing Time	10 min
Power Level	100%, 70%
Write Your Cooking Time Here	

* The duck should be left to dry for 1 to 2 hours before cooking.

Ingredients
1 duck, 1.5 to 2 kg (3-1/4 to 4-1/2 lb)
15 mL (1 tablespoon) honey
15 mL (1 tablespoon) water
5 mL (1 teaspoon) cider vinegar
2 cloves garlic, chopped
125 mL (1/2 cup) green onion, chopped
15 mL (1 tablespoon) soy sauce
30 mL (2 tablespoons) dry sherry
15 mL (1 tablespoon) powdered chicken concentrate
15 mL (1 tablespoon) ginger
5 mL (1 teaspoon) brown sugar
5 mL (1 teaspoon) oil
15 mL (1 tablespoon) butter
15 mL (1 tablespoon) wholewheat flour

Method
— Combine the honey, water and vinegar; cook at 100% for 1 minute and set aside.
— Wash the duck, pat dry, and let stand for 1 to 2 hours on a towel to dry thoroughly.
— Combine the garlic, green onion, soy sauce, sherry, chicken concentrate, ginger and brown sugar; mix well and heat at 100% for 1 minute.

⟹

Oriental Duck

Assemble all the ingredients for this oriental-style dish—typical fare from the Far East.

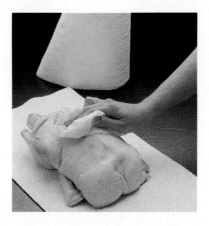

Dry the duck by patting it with a dry towel and then allowing it to stand for 1 to 2 hours.

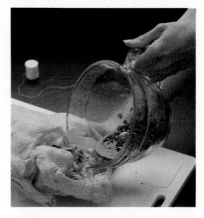

Put the cooked garlic and green onion mixture into the duck cavity and sew up the opening to retain both the juice and flavor during cooking.

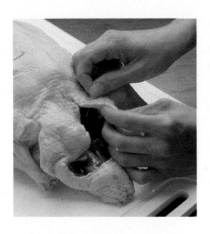

To sew the opening up, use a large needle with fine string and sew along the length.

Before cooking, baste the breast of the duck with the honey, water, and vinegar sauce.

To ensure even cooking, turn the duck over and rotate the dish halfway through the cooking time.

— Put this mixture into the duck cavity and sew up the opening.
— Preheat a browning dish at 100% for 7 minutes, add the oil, and heat at 100% for 30 seconds.
— Brown the breast of the duck and brush the skin with the honey sauce.
— Place the duck on a rack and cook at 70%, allowing 26 min/kg (12 min/lb).
— Halfway through the cooking time, give the dish a half-turn and turn the duck over. When the cooking period is over, allow the duck to stand for 10 minutes.
— Pour the cooking juices into a bowl and set aside.
— Heat the butter at 100% for 30 seconds, add the flour, and mix well. Add the cooking juices to the roux and heat at 100% for about 2 minutes, until the mixture thickens, stirring once.
— Serve the sauce with the duck.

Duck with Olives

Ingredients
1 duck, 2.25 kg (5 lb)
2 onions, thinly sliced
1 carrot, cut into sticks
30 mL (2 tablespoons) butter
1 bouquet garni

salt and pepper to taste
500 mL (2 cups) hot beef consommé
1 red pepper, diced
12 stuffed green olives

Level of Difficulty	🍴🍴
Preparation Time	10 min
Cost per Serving	$ $ $
Number of Servings	4
Nutritional Value	348 calories 36.9 g protein 18.4 g lipids
Food Exchanges	4 oz meat 1-1/2 fat exchanges 1 vegetable exchange
Cooking Time	33 min/kg (15 min/lb) + 5 min
Standing Time	None
Power Level	100%, 70%
Write Your Cooking Time Here	

Method
— Put the onions, carrots, and butter in a dish. Cover and cook at 100% for 2 to 3 minutes.
— Add the bouquet garni and season with salt.
— Prick the duck with a fork and season with pepper.
— Place the duck on the vegetables, breast side up; cover and cook at 70%, allowing 33 min/kg (15 min/lb).
— Halfway through the cooking time turn the duck over, add the consommé, cover and continue to cook.
— Remove the duck from the dish and set aside.
— Strain the consommé through a sieve to remove most of the fat, add the diced red pepper and olives, and cook at 100% for 1 to 2 minutes.
— Serve the duck on the bed of vegetables and olives and pour the liquid over it.

Quails with Onion

Level of Difficulty	¶¶
Preparation Time	15 min
Cost per Serving	$ $
Number of Servings	4
Nutritional Value	521 calories 25.6 g protein 43.6 g lipids
Food Exchanges	4 oz meat 1 fat exchange 1 vegetable exchange
Cooking Time	38 min
Standing Time	None
Power Level	100%, 70%
Write Your Cooking Time Here	

Ingredients
8 quails
175 mL (3/4 cup) lean bacon, diced
16 pearl onions, peeled
pepper to taste
30 mL (2 tablespoons) white wine

Method
— Wash the quails well and truss them.
— Put the diced bacon in a dish and cook at 100% for 2 to 3 minutes, stirring once.
— Add the onions, cover, and continue to cook at 100% for 2 to 3 minutes, or until the bacon is done.
— Arrange the quails in the dish, breast side down; season with pepper and cook at 70% for 15 minutes.
— Turn the quails over and continue to cook at 70% for another 15 minutes, or until the quails are done.
— Remove the quails from the oven, take them out of the dish, and cover with aluminum foil to keep them warm.
— Pour the white wine into the dish with the bacon and onions, and deglaze it; heat at 100% for 1 to 2 minutes.
— Pour the sauce over the quails and serve.

Quails with White Wine

Level of Difficulty	
Preparation Time	15 min
Cost per Serving	$ $ $
Number of Servings	4
Nutritional Value	341 calories 30.4 g protein 13.9 g lipids
Food Exchanges	3.5 oz meat 1 fat exchange 1 vegetable exchanges 1/2 bread exchange
Cooking Time	39 min
Standing Time	4 min
Power Level	100%, 70%
Write Your Cooking Time Here	

Ingredients
8 quails
pepper to taste
45 mL (3 tablespoons) butter
250 mL (1 cup) carrot, diced
1 onion, diced
2 green peppers, diced
1 284 mL (10 oz) can mushrooms, drained
30 mL (2 tablespoons) flour
175 mL (3/4 cup) chicken stock
125 mL (1/2 cup) white wine

Method
— Season the quails with pepper and truss them so that they keep their shape during cooking.
— Preheat a browning dish at 100% for 7 minutes; add 15 mL (1 tablespoon) butter and heat at 100% for 30 seconds.
— Brown the breasts of the quails in the hot butter and set aside.
— Add the remaining butter, carrots, onion, green peppers and mushrooms to the browning dish; cover and cook at 100% for 4 to 5 minutes, stirring after 3 minutes.
— Dredge with the flour and mix well.
— Add the chicken stock and white wine, heat at 100% for 3 to 4 minutes, or until the mixture thickens, stirring after 2 minutes.
— Put the quails in the sauce, breast side down; cover and cook at 70% for 15 minutes.
— Turn the quails over, cover, and cook at 70% for 12 to 15 minutes longer, or until the quails are tender.
— Allow to stand for 4 minutes before serving.

Season the quails with pepper and truss them before you brown them.

Cook the carrots, onion, peppers and mushrooms together. Halfway through the cooking time, dredge them with flour and add the wine and stock. Heat until the mixture thickens.

Cover the quails and cook them in the sauce. Turn them over halfway through the cooking time.

Crumb Coatings

For chicken pieces with a crunchy, golden crust, nothing is better than a good crumb coating. Whether you choose to buy one of the commercial coatings or to make your own, the result is sure to please your guests. Also, your choice of coating enables you to vary the taste of a poultry dish without changing the method of cooking it. Another advantage in using a crumb coating is that it prevents lean parts from overcooking and drying out.

A variety of ingredients, such as salted crackers, cereal, stale bread, graham crumbs, can be used in a crumb coating. You are limited only by your own preferences and your imagination. The flavor of a crumb coating can be enhanced by adding such ingredients as sesame seeds, poppy seeds, and herbs. If the amount of fat in your diet is a concern, remove the skin, which contains the most fat, from the poultry piece before coating it with crumbs. For a quick and healthy meal or snack, serve breaded chicken pieces with raw or cooked broccoli or with a salad.

Breaded Chicken Drumsticks—with Style

There is absolutely no reason why you have to follow established conventions in cooking. In fact, chicken goes very well with some rather exotic coating combinations. Seasoned crumb coatings enhance both the appearance and the flavor of chicken. Here are five of countless options.

Poppy Seed Coating

Add 10 mL (2 teaspoons) of poppy seeds to about 90 g (3 oz) of your chosen crumb base. Halfway through the cooking time, sprinkle the drumsticks with garlic salt.

Sesame Seed Coating

Mix 10 to 15 mL (2 to 3 teaspoons) of sesame seeds with 90 g (3 oz) of your chosen crumb base. You can also sprinkle the drumsticks with garlic salt or celery salt if you wish.

Fine Herbs Coating

If you like garlic, crush a clove and add it to 100 g (3-1/2 oz) of crumbs that you have seasoned with parsley and thyme.

Coconut Coating

If you would like something different, add a little interest to your meal by coating drumsticks with coconut. Add 25 mL (5 teaspoons) of dessicated coconut and 10 mL (2 teaspoons) of dried parsley to 90 g (3 oz) of your chosen crumb base. Season to taste.

Tarragon and Onion Coating

Add 5 mL (1 teaspoon) of chopped fresh tarragon and 15 mL (1 tablespoon) of thinly sliced onion to 90 g (3 oz) of your chosen crumb base. Season to taste.

How to Coat Pieces of Poultry

Crumb coatings play a dual role in cooking chicken. On the one hand, they enhance the appearance of the dish and so impress your guests right away. On the other, they add a distinctive flavor. To make the most of this technique, here are a few tips on how to coat chicken pieces.

Coating Ingredients

Before you coat chicken pieces in crumbs, dip them in beaten egg. The egg dip ensures that the crumbs will adhere well and it enriches the taste to some extent.

The chicken pieces can be dipped in milk instead of egg before coating. Milk is lighter than beaten egg or oil and has a less pronounced taste. However, it should be noted that the crumbs do not adhere as well.

Dipping the chicken pieces in oil before coating with crumbs also gives excellent results. The flavor will vary, depending on the type of oil used, but in most cases it will not overpower the flavor of the chicken.

Coating Techniques

Since the introduction of commercial crumb coatings, the bag technique has increased in popularity. Simply put the dipped chicken piece into a plastic bag containing the crumbs, hold the bag loosely, and shake well.

A much simpler but equally effective technique involves putting the crumbs on a plate and rolling the dipped pieces of meat in them.

Another approach is to shake the crumbs onto the piece of poultry. Put the meat on a dish to catch the excess crumbs.

Quail Casserole with Peas

Ingredients
4 quails
3 slices bacon, cut into four
115 g (4 oz) ground veal
115 g (4 oz) ham, cut in strips

1/2 onion, sliced
115 g (4 oz) mushrooms, sliced
1 225 g (8 oz) package frozen peas, defrosted
50 mL (1/4 cup) white wine

125 mL (1/2 cup) chicken stock

Level of Difficulty	🍴🍴
Preparation Time	15 min
Cost per Serving	$ $
Number of Servings	4
Nutritional Value	510 calories 51.3 g protein 20.1 g lipids
Food Exchanges	4.5 oz meat 2 fat exchanges 3 vegetable exchanges
Cooking Time	32 min
Standing Time	3 min
Power Level	100%, 70%
Write Your Cooking Time Here	

Method
— Rinse the quails thoroughly and truss them.
— Cook the bacon in a dish at 100% for 3 to 4 minutes.
— Add the ground veal and cook at 100% for 3 minutes, stirring twice to break up the meat.
— Add the remaining ingredients, mix well, and heat at 100% for 2 to 3 minutes, stirring after 1 minute.
— Lay the quails on this mixture, cover, and cook at 70% for 10 minutes.
— Turn the quails over, cover again, and cook at 70% for another 10 to 12 minutes.
— Allow to stand for 3 minutes before serving.

Cornish Game Hens with Black Cherries

Level of Difficulty	🍴🍴
Preparation Time	10 min
Cost per Serving	$ $
Number of Servings	4
Nutritional Value	374 calories 41.9 g protein 23 g lipids
Food Exchanges	4.5 oz meat 1 fat exchange 1 fruit exchange
Cooking Time	28 min
Standing Time	None
Power Level	100%, 70%
Write Your Cooking Time Here	

Ingredients
2 Cornish game hens, 675 g
(1-1/2 lb) each
30 mL (2 tablespoons) butter
30 mL (2 tablespoons) oil
salt and freshly ground
pepper to taste
1 398 mL (14 oz) can pitted
black cherries
125 mL (1/2 cup) chicken
stock

Method
— Wash the birds thoroughly
and truss them.
— Preheat a browning dish
at 100% for 7 minutes;
add the oil and butter and
heat at 100% for 30
seconds.
— Brown the birds in the hot
oil and butter.
— Cover the dish and cook
the birds at 70% for 10
minutes.
— Baste the birds with their
cooking juices and
rearrange them so that
those parts facing the
center now face the outer
edge of the dish.
— Season with salt and
pepper, leave uncovered,
and cook at 70% for 15
minutes.
— Arrange the birds on a
serving dish. Set aside.
— Deglaze the pan by adding
the cherries with 45 mL (3
tablespoons) of their syrup
and the chicken stock and
mixing well. Cook at
100% for 2 to 3 minutes,
stirring after 1 minute.
— Pour the sauce over the
hens and serve on a bed
of noodles.

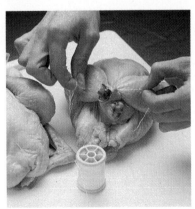

Clean the Cornish game hens and then truss them so that they keep their shape during the cooking process.

Brown the birds in the hot oil and butter to give them an attractive golden appearance.

During the cooking period, change the position of the birds in the dish to ensure even cooking.

Cornish Game Hens with Sausage Stuffing

Level of Difficulty	
Preparation Time	15 min
Cost per Serving	$ $
Number of Servings	4
Nutritional Value	539 calories 52.5 g protein 27 g lipids
Food Exchanges	5 oz meat 1/2 bread exchange 2 fat exchanges
Cooking Time	35 min
Standing Time	None
Power Level	70%, 90%, 100%
Write Your Cooking Time Here	

Ingredients
2 Cornish game hens, 675 g (1-1/2 lb) each
salt and pepper to taste
15 mL (1 tablespoon) butter
paprika to taste
30 mL (2 tablespoons) chicken powder concentrate
250 mL (1 cup) chicken stock
1 onion, chopped
4 chicken livers, ground
450 g (1 lb) smoked sausage, sliced
4 slices toast, diced

Method
— Season the cavities of the birds with salt and pepper.
— Combine the butter, paprika and the chicken concentrate and brush over the birds.
— Put the birds on a rack, breast side down; add the chicken stock and cook at 70% for 10 minutes.
— Turn the birds over and continue to cook at 70% for 15 minutes longer, or until they are done.
— Take the birds out of the oven, put them on a plate, and cover with aluminum foil, putting the shiny side next to the meat.
— Allow the cooking juices to cool and skim off the fat.
— Put the onion and ground chicken livers in a dish; cover and cook at 90% for 3 to 4 minutes, stirring after 2 minutes.
— Add the sausages, the diced toast and the cooking juices.
— Cover and heat at 100% for 4 to 6 minutes, stirring every 2 minutes.
— Arrange the stuffing on a platter, place the birds on top, and serve.

Brush the Cornish game hens with the mixture of butter and chicken powder concentrate before putting them in the oven.

When the birds are done, put them on a plate and allow the cooking juices to cool so that you can skim off the fat more easily.

Cook the onion and ground chicken livers together, stirring the mixture after 2 minutes to ensure even cooking.

Chicken with Garlic

Level of Difficulty	🍴
Preparation Time	10 min
Cost per Serving	$
Number of Servings	6
Nutritional Value	363 calories 41.3 g protein 16.4 g lipids
Food Exchanges	5 oz meat 1-1/2 fat exchanges
Cooking Time	22 min/kg (10 min/lb)
Standing Time	5 min
Power Level	70%
Write Your Cooking Time Here	

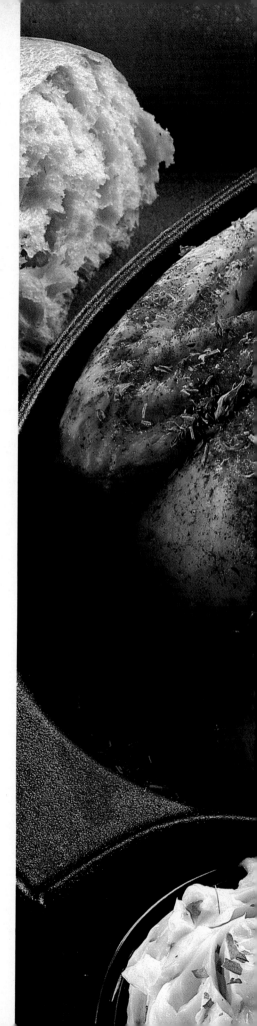

Ingredients
1 chicken, 2 kg (4-1/2 lb)
1 bouquet garni
pepper and paprika to taste
75 mL (1/3 cup) oil
40 cloves garlic
a few pinches rosemary,
thyme and sage
15 mL (1 tablespoon) parsley

Method
— Put the bouquet garni in the cavity of the chicken.
— Rub the chicken with the pepper and paprika.
— Put the oil, whole cloves of garlic, rosemary, thyme, sage and parsley in a deep dish.
— Put the chicken in the dish, breast side down, and cover; cook at 70% allowing 22 min/kg (10 min/lb).
— After 20 minutes cooking time, turn the chicken over to ensure even cooking.
— Allow to stand for 5 minutes and serve with garlic bread.

Chicken Breasts with Pistachios

Level of Difficulty	
Preparation Time	10 min
Cost per Serving	$ $
Number of Servings	4
Nutritional Value	503 calories 35.2 g protein 34.7 g lipids
Food Exchanges	4.5 oz meat 3 fat exchanges 1 bread exchange
Cooking Time	25 min
Standing Time	None
Power Level	100%, 70%
Write Your Cooking Time Here	

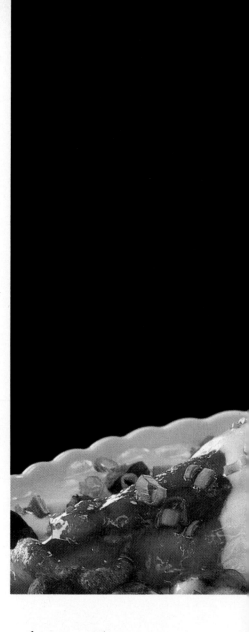

Ingredients
2 whole chicken breasts, cut in half
45 mL (3 tablespoons) wholewheat flour
salt and white pepper to taste
30 mL (2 tablespoons) butter
50 mL (1/4 cup) dry white wine
250 mL (1 cup) 35% cream
15 mL (1 tablespoon) brandy
30 mL (2 tablespoons) pistachios, coarsely chopped
15 mL (1 tablespoon) green onion, finely chopped

Method
— Mix the flour and pepper and coat the breasts with it.
— Preheat a browning dish at 100% for 7 minutes; add the butter and heat at 100% for 30 seconds.
— Brown the chicken breasts in the hot butter; sprinkle with the white wine, cover, and cook at 70% for 18 to 22 minutes.
— Halfway through the cooking time, give the dish a half-turn.
— Remove the breasts from the oven and put on a separate plate. Set aside.
— Add the cream to the cooking juices and heat at 100% for 2 to 3 minutes, stirring every minute.
— Add the brandy and the pistachios and season to taste.
— Coat the breasts with the sauce and garnish with the chopped green onion before serving.

Coat the breasts with the wholewheat flour and then brown them in hot butter to give them an attractive golden appearance.

Sprinkle the wine over the breasts and cook covered so that the meat takes on the special flavor of the wine.

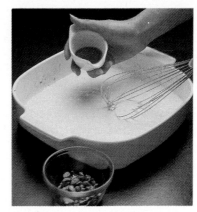

Add the brandy and the pistachios to the cooking juices and the cream and pour the sauce generously over the breasts. Irresistible!

Chicken Parmesan

Level of Difficulty	
Preparation Time	10 min
Cost per Serving	$ $
Number of Servings	6
Nutritional Value	348 calories 41 g protein 14 g lipids
Food Exchanges	5 oz meat 1 vegetable exchange 1/2 bread exchange
Cooking Time	34 min
Standing Time	None
Power Level	70%, 90%
Write Your Cooking Time Here	

Ingredients
3 whole chicken breasts, cut in half
1 package crumb coating
50 mL (1/4 cup) Parmesan cheese, grated
1 398 mL (14 oz) can Italian–style tomato sauce
250 mL (1 cup) mozzarella cheese, grated
paprika to garnish

Method
— Coat the chicken breasts with the crumbs and sprinkle them with the Parmesan cheese.
— Place the breasts on a rack and cook at 70% for 15 minutes.
— Turn the breasts over and cook at 70% for another 14 to 16 minutes.
— Pour the tomato sauce into a dish, place the breasts in the sauce, cover with the mozzarella cheese, and sprinkle with paprika.
— Cook at 90% for 2 to 3 minutes, or until the cheese has melted.

Assemble all the ingredients for this typically Italian dish.

Coat the breasts with the crumbs and sprinkle with Parmesan cheese.

After the first cooking period, turn the breasts over to ensure even cooking.

Lay the breasts in the tomato sauce and heat until the mozzarella cheese in completely melted.

Chicken Italian Style

Level of Difficulty	
Preparation Time	15 min
Cost per Serving	$ $
Number of Servings	6
Nutritional Value	350 calories 41 g protein 15 g lipids
Food Exchanges	5 oz meat 1-1/2 vegetable exchanges 1/2 bread exchange
Cooking Time	38 min
Standing Time	None
Power Level	70%, 100%, 90%
Write Your Cooking Time Here	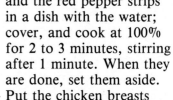

Ingredients
3 whole chicken breasts, boned, skinned, and cut in half
1 package Italian crumb coating
50 mL (1/4 cup) Parmesan cheese, grated
175 mL (3/4 cup) mozzarella cheese, grated
paprika to garnish
500 mL (2 cups) broccoli flowerets
75 mL (1/3 cup) water
1/2 red pepper, cut into strips

Method
— Coat the chicken breasts with the crumbs and the Parmesan cheese.
— Place them on a rack with the thicker parts facing the outside, leave uncovered, and cook at 70% for 15 minutes.
— Turn the breasts over, leave uncovered, and cook at 70% for another 14 to 16 minutes, or until the meat is tender.
— Top the breasts with the mozzarella cheese, sprinkle with the paprika, and set aside.
— Put the broccoli flowerets and the red pepper strips in a dish with the water; cover, and cook at 100% for 2 to 3 minutes, stirring after 1 minute. When they are done, set them aside.
— Put the chicken breasts back in the oven and heat at 90% for 3 to 4 minutes, or until the cheese is completely melted.
— Serve the chicken with the broccoli and the strips of red pepper.

MICROTIPS

How To Make Breadcrumbs

To make your own breadcrumbs, break 3 slices of bread into pieces, put them on a microwave-safe dish, and dry them in the oven at 100% for 2 to 3 minutes. Allow them to cool for 10 minutes and then crush them.

Freezing Breaded Drumsticks

Drumsticks that are cooked in a crumb coating can be kept in the freezer for 4 months. They will still be crisp and tasty when you reheat them in the microwave.

How To Clarify Butter

Put 60 mL (4 tablespoons) of butter in a glass measuring cup and heat at 100% for 1 to 1-1/2 minutes. Remove from the oven and skim off the fatty material that has floated to the top. Discard the milky liquid in the bottom of the cup.

Roast Chicken with Oregano

Level of Difficulty	🍴
Preparation Time	15 min
Cost per Serving	$
Number of Servings	4
Nutritional Value	371 calories 35 g protein 30 g lipids
Food Exchanges	5 oz meat 3 fat exchanges
Cooking Time	22 min/kg (10 min/lb)
Standing Time	6 min
Power Level	70%
Write Your Cooking Time Here	

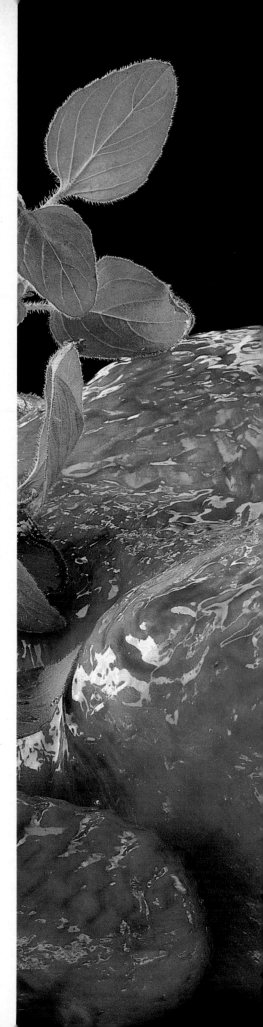

Ingredients
1 chicken, 1.3 kg (3 lb)
salt and pepper to taste
60 mL (4 tablespoons) olive oil
45 mL (3 tablespoons) lemon juice
7 mL (1/2 tablespoon) oregano
30 mL (2 tablespoons) chicken powder concentrate
paprika to taste

Method
— Season the inside of the bird with salt and pepper, and the outside with pepper only.
— Combine all the other ingredients and mix well.
— Baste the chicken with some of the mixture.
— Put the chicken on a rack, leave uncovered, and cook at 70%, allowing 22 min/kg (10 min/lb).
— Halfway through the cooking time, baste the chicken with the remainder of the mixture and give the rack a half-turn.
— Allow to stand for 6 minutes before serving.

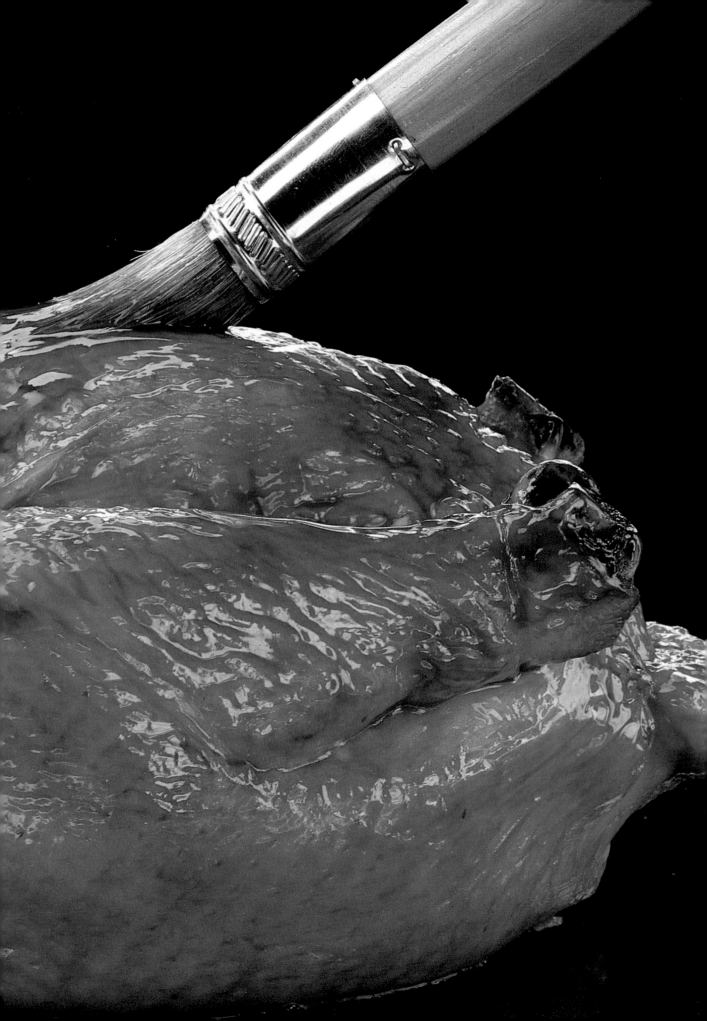

Chicken in Champagne

Level of Difficulty	
Preparation Time	20 min
Cost per Serving	$ $
Number of Servings	6
Nutritional Value	483 calories 46.2 g protein 25.4 g lipids
Food Exchanges	5 oz meat 3 fat exchanges 2 vegetable exchanges
Cooking Time	52 min
Standing Time	None
Power Level	100%, 70%
Write Your Cooking Time Here	

Ingredients
1 chicken, 1.8 kg (4 lb), cut into serving pieces, or 8 chicken pieces
2 mL (1/2 teaspoon) black pepper
30 mL (2 tablespoons) butter
2 onions, thinly sliced
30 mL (2 tablespoons) brandy
125 mL (1/2 cup) chicken stock
125 mL (1/2 cup) champagne
2 mL (1/2 teaspoon) dried thyme
1 mL (1/4 teaspoon) ground mace
1 bay leaf
45 mL (3 tablespoons) flour
125 mL (1/2 cup) 35% cream
175 g (6 oz) mushrooms, washed and cut into thin strips
2 mL (1/2 teaspoon) cornstarch dissolved in 5 mL (1 teaspoon) water

Method
— Season the chicken pieces with the pepper and set aside.
— Put the butter in a dish and heat at 100% for 40 seconds; add the onions, cover, and cook at 100% for 2 to 3 minutes.
— Add the chicken, cover, and cook at 70% for 20 minutes, giving the dish a half-turn halfway through the cooking time.
— Take the dish out of the oven, remove the chicken pieces, and set aside.
— Pour the brandy, chicken stock, and champagne into the dish in which the chicken was cooked; add the thyme, mace, bay leaf, and flour and mix well.
— Add the cream and mushrooms.
— Cook at 100% for 5 to 6 minutes, until the sauce thickens, stirring every 2

minutes.
— Add the chicken to the sauce, cover, and cook at 70% for 15 to 20 minutes, or until the meat is tender.
— Remove the chicken pieces from the cooking dish and place them on a serving platter.
— Add the dissolved cornstarch to the sauce and heat at 100% for 2 to 3 minutes, or until the sauce thickens, stirring every minute.
— Pour the sauce over the chicken and serve.

MICROTIPS

Roasting a Whole Chicken

To ensure that the bird cooks evenly, give the dish a half-turn halfway through the cooking time and turn the bird over about three-quarters of the way through the cooking time. Let the bird stand for ten minutes before serving to allow even distribution of the heat.

To ensure that the bird cooks evenly, give the dish a half turn halfway through the cooking time and turn the bird over about three-quarters of the way through the cooking time. Let the bird stand for ten minutes before serving to allow even distribution of the heat.

Chicken Madeira

Level of Difficulty	
Preparation Time	20 min
Cost per Serving	$ $
Number of Servings	6
Nutritional Value	260 calories 33.5 g protein 8.4 g lipids
Food Exchanges	4 oz meat 1 vegetable exchange
Cooking Time	27 min
Standing Time	3 min
Power Level	100%, 70%
Write Your Cooking Time Here	

Ingredients
3 whole chicken breasts, boned, skinned, and cut in half
15 mL (1 tablespoon) butter
125 mL (1/2 cup) green onion, thinly sliced
225 g (8 oz) fresh mushrooms, sliced
50 mL (1/4 cup) Madeira wine
5 mL (1 teaspoon) tarragon
pepper to taste

Method
— Place the chicken breasts between two sheets of waxed paper and flatten them with the palm of your hand.
— Roll the breasts up, secure them with string or a toothpick, and set aside.
— Put the butter in a dish and heat at 100% for 30 seconds.
— Add the green onion and mushrooms, cover, and cook at 100% for 2 to 3 minutes, stirring once.
— Add the Madeira, tarragon, and pepper and mix well; cook at 100% for 2 minutes.
— Place the rolled breasts in the same dish, adding more Madeira if necessary, and cook at 70% for 18 to 22 minutes, rearranging them halfway through the cooking time.
— Allow to stand for 3 minutes.
— Coat with the Madeira, top with onions and mushrooms, and serve.

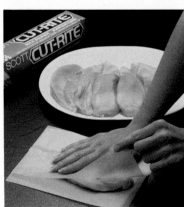

Place the breasts between two sheets of waxed paper and flatten them with the palm of your hand.

Roll up the breasts and secure them with string or a toothpick.

To ensure even cooking, rearrange the rolled breasts halfway through the cooking time.

Chicken Breasts Divan

Level of Difficulty	🍴
Preparation Time	15 min
Cost per Serving	$ $
Number of Servings	4
Nutritional Value	361 calories 40.7 g protein 16.1 g lipids
Food Exchanges	4.5 oz meat 1 fat exchange 1 vegetable exchange
Cooking Time	27 min
Standing Time	3 min
Power Level	70%, 100%
Write Your Cooking Time Here	

Ingredients
2 whole chicken breasts, boned, skinned, and cut in half
1 284 mL (10 oz) can cream of chicken soup
1 284 mL (10 oz) can cream of mushroom soup
5 mL (1 teaspoon) lemon juice
1 head broccoli
salt and pepper to taste
50 mL (1/4 cup) Parmesan cheese, grated

Method
— Put the chicken breasts in a dish, cover them, and cook at 70% for 13 to 16 minutes, or until the meat is tender, rearranging them halfway through the cooking time.
— Cut the breasts into large chunks and set aside.
— Combine the cream of chicken soup, cream of mushroom soup, lemon juice, and the cooking juices. Mix well and set aside.
— Trim and wash the broccoli, put into a dish with a little water, cover, and cook at 100% for 4 to 6 minutes, stirring halfway through the cooking time.
— Drain the broccoli and add it to the sauce; add the chicken, season to taste, and heat at 70% for 4 to 5 minutes, giving the dish a half-turn halfway through the cooking time.
— Sprinkle with the Parmesan cheese, cover, and allow to stand for 3 minutes before serving.

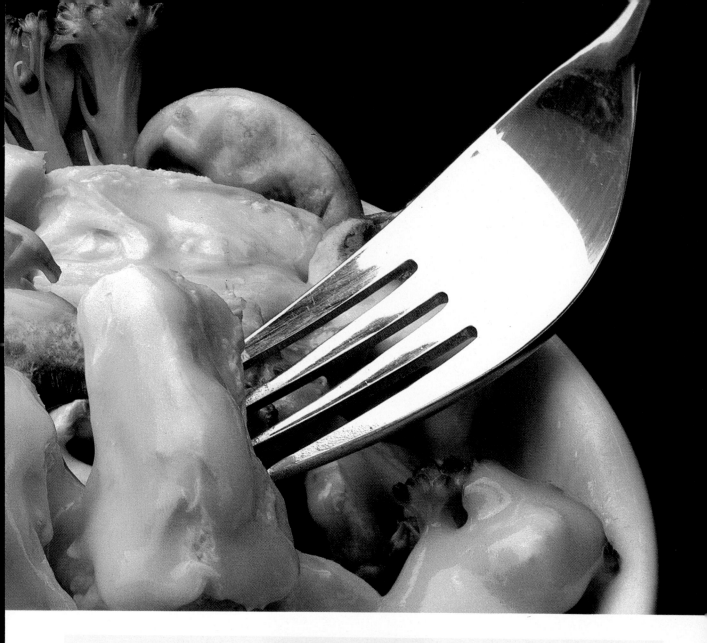

MICROTIPS

How To Cook Broccoli

Broccoli makes a delicious vegetable to accompany any meal and is easy to prepare in the microwave. To cook fresh broccoli, place 225 g (8 oz) flowerets in a shallow dish with the stems facing outward and add 60 mL (4 tablespoons) water. Cover with plastic wrap,

leaving a small opening, and cook at 100% for 3 to 5 minutes, giving the dish a half-turn once.

Serve hot with melted butter.

To cook frozen broccoli, place 225 g (8 oz) broccoli flowerets in a shallow dish and add 30 mL (2 tablespoons) water. Cover with plastic wrap, leaving a small opening, and cook at 100% for 2 minutes. Separate the flowerets from each other and cook for 3 to 4 minutes longer. Serve hot with melted butter.

Chicken Breasts with Peaches

Ingredients

2 whole chicken breasts,
boned and cut in half
30 mL (2 tablespoons) butter
1 284 mL (10 oz) can chicken
broth
15 mL (1 tablespoon)
Worcestershire sauce
1 mL (1/4 teaspoon) ginger
30 mL (2 tablespoons) green
onion, chopped
1 398 mL (14 oz) can sliced
peaches, drained
15 mL (1 tablespoon)
cornstarch dissolved in
30 mL (2 tablespoons) water

Method

— Preheat a browning dish
at 100% for 7 minutes;
add the butter and heat at
100% for 30 seconds.
— Brown the breasts in the
hot butter.
— Add the chicken broth,
Worcestershire sauce and
ginger; cover and cook at
70% for 7 minutes.
— Give the dish a half-turn
to ensure even cooking.
— Continue to cook at 70%
for another 5 to 7
minutes, or until the meat
is tender.
— Remove the chicken from
the dish and set aside.
— Add the green onion,
peaches and dissolved
cornstarch to the cooking
juices and mix well.
— Heat at 100% for 2 to 3
minutes, stirring every
minute.
— Pour the sauce over the
chicken and serve.

Chicken with Sautéed Vegetables

Ingredients
2 whole chicken breasts,
boned and skinned
30 mL (2 tablespoons) oil
50 mL (1/4 cup) onion,
thinly sliced
250 mL (1 cup) carrots, cut
into thin strips
125 mL (1/2 cup) celery,
sliced diagonally
2 mL (1/2 teaspoon)
rosemary
pepper to taste
250 mL (1 cup) mushrooms,
sliced
1 284 mL (10 oz) can chicken
broth
22 mL (1-1/2 tablespoons)
cornstarch

Method
— Cut the chicken breasts
into cubes and set aside.
— Put the oil, onion, carrot
sticks, celery, rosemary,
and pepper into a dish;
cover and cook at 100%
for 6 to 7 minutes, stirring
halfway through the
cooking time.
— Add the mushrooms,
cover, and set aside.
— Pour the chicken broth
into another dish, dissolve
the cornstarch in it, and
heat at 100% for 2 to 3
minutes, or until the broth
thickens.
— Add the chicken and
vegetables to the broth,
cover and cook at 70%
for 7 minutes; stir, and
cook for 7 to 9 minutes
longer.
— Allow to stand for 3
minutes before serving.

Chicken Croissant

Level of Difficulty	🍴
Preparation Time	10 min
Cost per Serving	**$**
Number of Servings	4
Nutritional Value	256 calories 13.5 g protein 16.2 g lipids
Food Exchanges	1.5 oz meat 2 fat exchanges 1 bread exchange
Cooking Time	12 min
Standing Time	None
Power Level	70%, 100%
Write Your Cooking Time Here	

Ingredients
1/2 chicken breast
4 slices bacon, cut in two
4 croissants, cut in half
60 mL (4 tablespoons) mayonnaise
4 slices tomato
4 lettuce leaves
pepper to taste

Method
— Put the chicken breast in a dish, cover, and cook at 70% for 5 to 7 minutes, giving the dish a half-turn halfway through the cooking time.
— When the chicken is cold, cut it into 4 slices.
— Place the bacon on a rack, cover with paper towel, and cook at 100% for 4 to 5 minutes, or until done to your liking.
— Spread mayonnaise on each of four croissant halves and add a portion of chicken, bacon, tomato and lettuce. Season with pepper and put the other half of the croissant on top to make a sandwich.

Hot Chicken Sandwich

Level of Difficulty	
Preparation Time	15 min
Cost per Serving	**$**
Number of Servings	4
Nutritional Value	543 calories 55.6 g protein 14.4 g lipids
Food Exchanges	5 oz meat 1/2 fat exchange 2 vegetable exchanges 2 bread exchanges
Cooking Time	39 min (+ 2 min per serving)
Standing Time	None
Power Level	70%, 100%, 90%
Write Your Cooking Time Here	

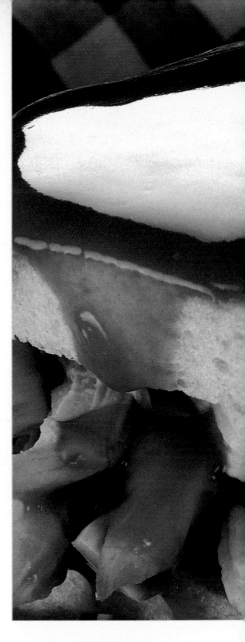

Ingredients
1 chicken, 1.3 kg (3 lb)
salt and pepper to taste
1 package sauce mix for hot chicken sandwich
500 mL (2 cups) frozen peas, defrosted
8 slices bread

Method
— Wash the chicken, dry well, and season the cavity with salt and pepper.
— Place the chicken on a rack, breast side down, cover, and cook at 70% for 15 minutes.
— Turn the chicken over, cover, and cook at 70% for another 15 minutes, or until the chicken is done.
— Take the chicken out of the oven and allow to cool a little; carve the meat from the bones and set aside.
— Follow the directions on the package to make the sauce. Heat at 100% for 4 to 5 minutes, stirring every 2 minutes.
— Heat the peas at 90% for 3 to 4 minutes, stirring at least once.
— Lay a slice of bread on a plate and top with chicken; cover with another slice of bread, and pour the hot sauce over the sandwich.
— Place the sandwich in the oven at 90% for 1 to 2 minutes.
— Make the other sandwiches in the same way.
— Serve on individual plates with peas.

MICROTIPS

To Tenderize Chicken

Pay close attention to the length of time you allow for cooking chicken. If you cook chicken for too long in the microwave it will become leathery. If you want really tender chicken, marinate it in the refrigerator for 24 hours before cooking.

You can make a simple marinade with equal parts of lemon juice (or white vinegar) and oil. Add herbs and seasoning to taste.

For Crispy Chicken

Here are two simple ways to make chicken pieces crispy.

1. Coat the pieces with egg and cracker crumbs before cooking them.

2. Remove the skin before cooking and brush the meat with a browning agent, such as soy sauce or Teriyaki sauce. Chicken prepared in this way will contain fewer calories than chicken with its skin.

Chicken Pies

Level of Difficulty	🍴🍴
Preparation Time	30 min
Cost per Serving	$
Number of Servings	4
Nutritional Value	529 calories 31.8 g protein 32.3 g lipids
Food Exchanges	3 oz meat 2 fat exchanges 2 vegetable exchanges 1-1/2 bread exchanges 1/2 milk exchange
Cooking Time	18 min (+ 4 min per serving)
Standing Time	2 min
Power Level	100%, 90%
Write Your Cooking Time Here	

Ingredients
Filling:
500 mL (2 cups) cooked chicken, cut into large dice
3 carrots, cut into small dice
2 potatoes, cut into small dice
60 mL (4 tablespoons) hot water
90 mL (6 tablespoons) butter
90 mL (6 tablespoons) flour
salt, pepper, and parsley to taste
30 mL (2 tablespoons) roasted red pepper, chopped
375 mL (1-1/2 cups) chicken stock
250 mL (1 cup) milk
1 284 mL (10 oz) can sliced mushrooms, drained
250 mL (1 cup) frozen peas
Pastry:
250 mL (1 cup) flour
10 mL (2 teaspoons) baking powder
2 mL (1/2 teaspoon) baking soda
2 mL (1/2 teaspoon) salt
30 mL (2 tablespoons) cold butter
125 mL (1/2 cup) cold milk
30 mL (2 tablespoons) melted butter
45 mL (3 tablespoons) fresh parsley, chopped
60 mL (4 tablespoons) Parmesan cheese, grated
paprika to garnish

Method
— Begin by making the filling. Put the carrots, potatoes, and hot water in a dish; cover and cook at 100% for 4 minutes.
— Rearrange the vegetables so that those in the center are now at the edges of the dish; cook at 100% for another 5 to 6 minutes, or until the vegetables are done, and set aside.
— In another dish melt the butter at 100% for 1

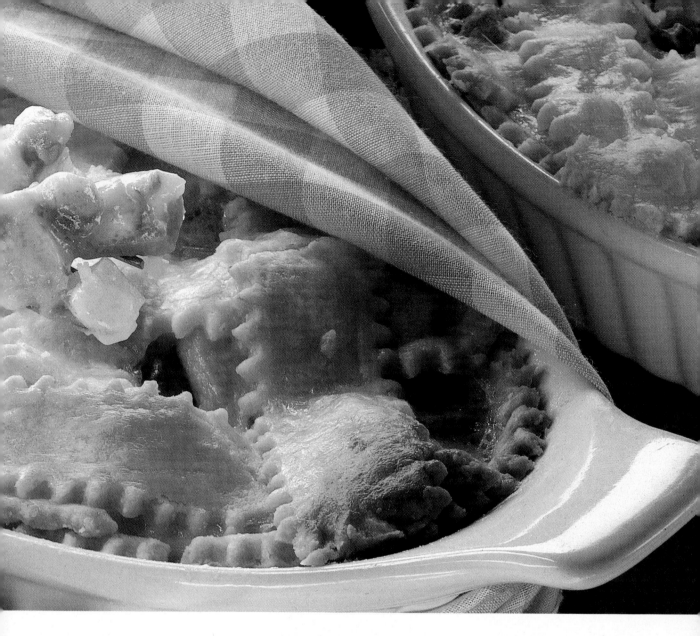

minute, add the flour and mix well.
— Add the salt, pepper, parsley and red pepper, and then add the chicken stock and milk. Mix well.
— Cook at 100% for 6 to 7 minutes, until the mixture thickens, stirring every 2 minutes.
— Add the chicken, cooked vegetables, mushrooms, and peas to the sauce; check the seasoning and set aside.
— Begin the pastry by combining the flour, baking powder, baking soda and salt in a large bowl.
— Rub the cold butter into the dry ingredients until the mixture resembles breadcrumbs; add the milk and mix well.
— Knead the pastry dough for a few minutes, roll out into a rectangle, and brush with the melted butter.
— Sprinkle the pastry with parsley and half of the Parmesan cheese, and cut it into strips.
— Spoon equal amounts of the filling into 4 au gratin dishes and arrange the strips of pastry on each.
— Sprinkle with paprika and the remaining Parmesan cheese. Cook each pie at 90% for 3 to 4 minutes, or until the pastry is done.
— Allow to stand for 2 minutes before serving.

Chicken Fricassee

Level of Difficulty	
Preparation Time	20 min
Cost per Serving	$
Number of Servings	4
Nutritional Value	239 calories 26.2 g protein 9.1 g lipids
Food Exchanges	3 oz meat 2 vegetable exchanges
Cooking Time	21 min
Standing Time	None
Power Level	100%, 90%, 70%
Write Your Cooking Time Here	

Ingredients
1 whole and 1 half chicken breast, boned, skinned, and cut into large dice
175 mL (3/4 cup) carrot, diced
175 mL (3/4 cup) potato, diced
175 mL (3/4 cup) rutabaga, diced
75 mL (1/3 cup) onion, thinly sliced
125 mL (1/2 cup) hot water
15 mL (1 tablespoon) parsley
5 mL (1 teaspoon) poultry seasoning
salt and pepper to taste
15 mL (1 tablespoon) butter
15 mL (1 tablespoon) flour

Method
— Put the vegetables in a dish with 75 mL (1/3 cup) water, cover the dish, and cook at 100% for 4 to 5 minutes, stirring halfway through the cooking time.
— Put the chicken in a deep dish and add the cooked vegetables, hot water, parsley, poultry seasoning, salt and pepper.
— Cover the dish and cook at 90% for 5 minutes; give the dish a half-turn, and continue to cook at 90% for 3 to 4 minutes longer or until the chicken is done. Remove the chicken and vegetables and set aside.
— Melt the butter in a measuring cup at 100% for 30 seconds; add the flour and mix well.
— Strain the cooking stock through a fine sieve, mix well with the roux and cook at 100% for 2 to 3 minutes until it thickens.
— Pour the resulting sauce over the mixture of chicken and vegetables and heat at 70% for 3 to 4 minutes, stirring once.

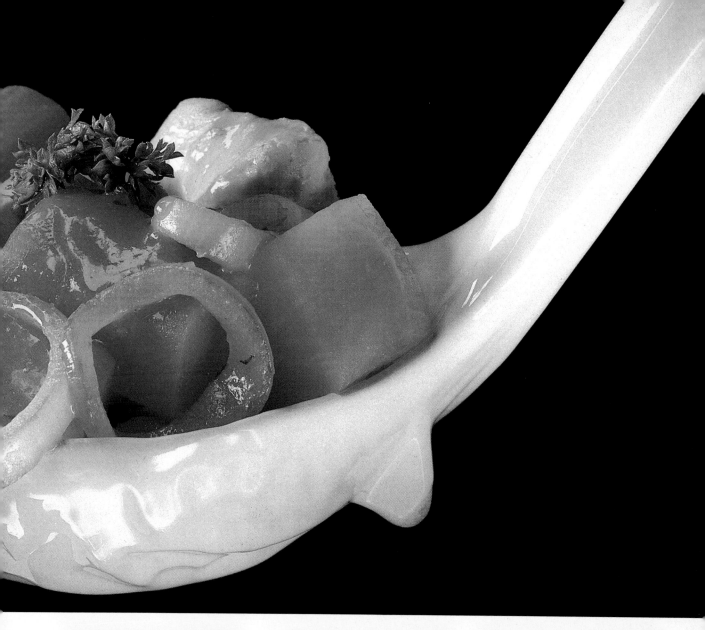

Assemble all the ingredients for this recipe, one that is sure to be a success with the family.

To ensure that the vegetables cook evenly, put those that cook more slowly toward the outside of the dish.

Put the chicken in a deep dish, cover with the vegetables and water, and cook as directed in the recipe.

Chicken Chasseur

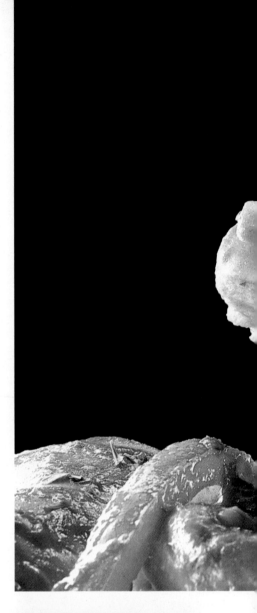

Level of Difficulty	🍴
Preparation Time	10 min
Cost per Serving	$
Number of Servings	6
Nutritional Value	273 calories 33.2 g protein 9.5 g lipids
Food Exchanges	3.5 oz meat 1/2 fat exchange 1 vegetable exchange
Cooking Time	40 min
Standing Time	5 min
Power Level	100%, 70%
Write Your Cooking Time Here	

Ingredients
1 chicken, about 1.3 kg (3 lb), skinned and cut into serving pieces
15 mL (1 tablespoon) butter
1 onion, chopped
1 green pepper, cut into strips
1 clove garlic, chopped
50 mL (1/4 cup) flour
1 796 mL (28 oz) can tomatoes
125 mL (1/2 cup) water
1 bay leaf
15 mL (1 tablespoon) parsley, chopped
salt and pepper to taste
oregano, paprika and basil to taste

Method
— Put the butter, onion, green pepper and garlic into a dish and cook at 100% for 4 to 5 minutes, stirring halfway through the cooking time.
— Add the flour and the tomatoes and stir well.
— Add the water, herbs and seasoning.
— Cook at 100% for 4 to 5 minutes, stirring once. Add the chicken pieces, cover the dish, and continue to cook at 70% for 25 to 30 minutes, stirring once.
— Allow to stand for 5 minutes before serving.

Assemble all the ingredients for this classic chicken dish.

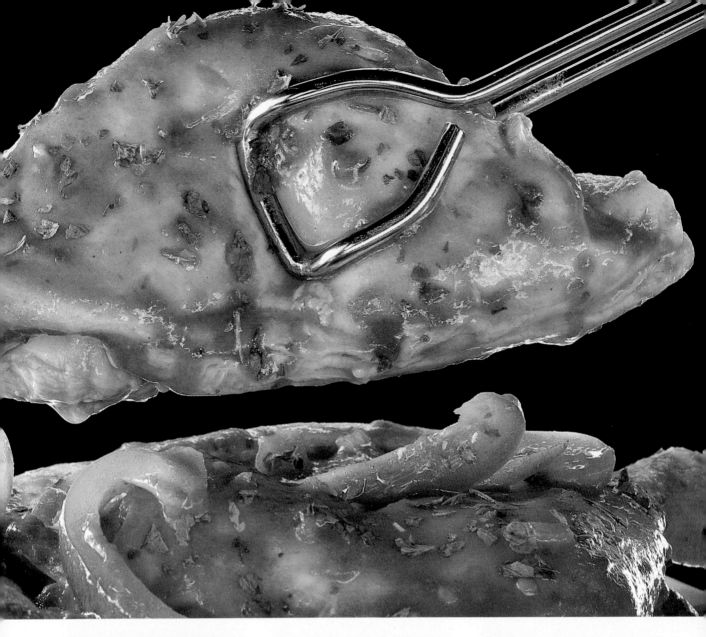

Add the flour and tomatoes to the onion, green pepper and garlic; mix well and then add the water and aromatic herbs.

Let the chicken simmer in the resulting sauce so that it takes on a subtle flavor.

To ensure even cooking, stir halfway through the cooking time.

Chicken Casserole

Level of Difficulty	🍴
Preparation Time	15 min
Cost per Serving	$ $
Number of Servings	6
Nutritional Value	311 calories 32.3 g protein 15.1 g lipids
Food Exchanges	4 oz meat 1 fat exchange 1 vegetable exchange
Cooking Time	26 min
Standing Time	4 min
Power Level	100%, 70%
Write Your Cooking Time Here	

Ingredients
1 chicken, 1.3 kg (3 lb), cut into serving pieces
60 mL (4 tablespoons) butter
125 mL (1/2 cup) onion, chopped
1 clove garlic, chopped
1 green pepper, diced
125 mL (1/2 cup) tomato paste
125 mL (1/2 cup) dry white wine
125 mL (1/2 cup) chicken stock
15 mL (1 tablespoon) parsley, chopped
salt and pepper to taste

Method
— Preheat a browning dish at 100% for 7 minutes; add the butter and heat at 100% for 30 seconds.
— Brown the chicken pieces in the hot butter, remove them, and set aside.
— Add the remaining ingredients to the dish, mix well, and cook at 100% for 5 to 6 minutes, stirring after 3 minutes.
— Place the chicken pieces in the dish and cook at 70% for 18 to 20 minutes, stirring halfway through the cooking time.
— Allow to stand for 4 minutes before serving.

Assemble all the ingredients for this simple and delicious recipe.

94

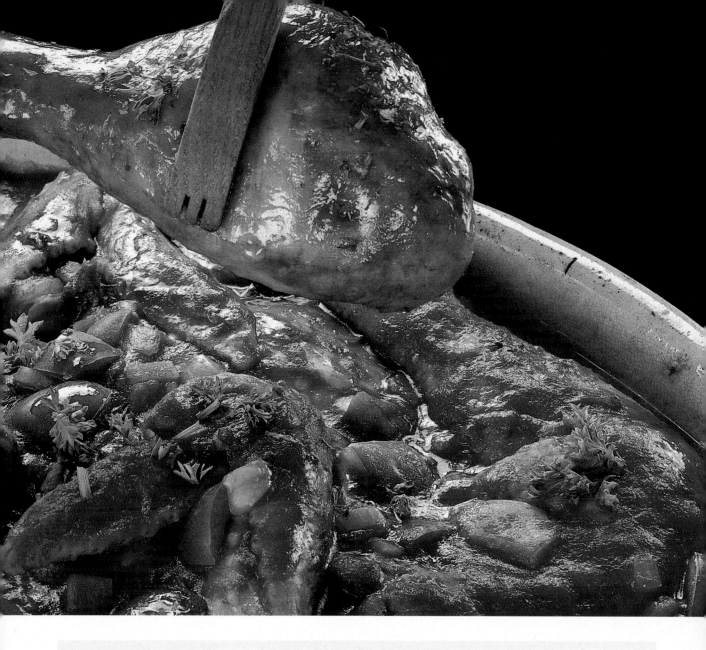

MICROTIPS

Defrosting Chicken Legs

When you buy frozen chicken legs, they are sometimes wrapped tightly together and cannot be separated before defrosting. To get around this problem, put the wrapped chicken legs in the microwave at 30% for a brief defrosting period. Then remove the wrapping and separate the legs. If you still cannot separate them, put the frozen block of meat back in the microwave for 2 minutes at a time, until you can. Arrange the legs in a circle on a bacon rack, taking care to place the thicker parts so that they face the outside of the rack. Divide the defrosting time in the microwave into four equal periods, alternating with standing periods equal to a quarter of the total defrosting time (see the chart on page 10). Halfway through the defrosting time, give the dish a half-turn to ensure even defrosting. At the end of the defrosting time, allow the legs to stand for 10 minutes, rinse them in cold water, and dry well before you cook them. When cooking chicken legs, arrange them on the dish as you did to defrost them.

Chicken with Sour Cream

Level of Difficulty	
Preparation Time	10 min
Cost per Serving	$ $
Number of Servings	6
Nutritional Value	310 calories 32.9 g protein 14.4 g lipids
Food Exchanges	4 oz meat 1 fat exchange 1 vegetable exchange
Cooking Time	21 min
Standing Time	None
Power Level	100%, 70%
Write Your Cooking Time Here	

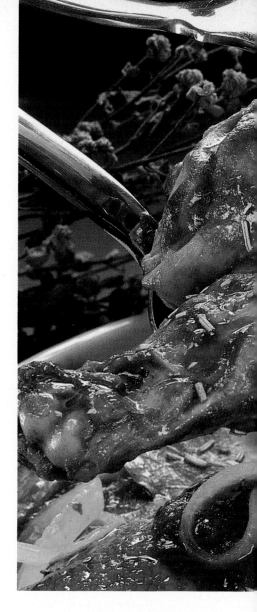

Ingredients
6 to 8 chicken pieces
30 mL (2 tablespoons) oil
1 onion, thinly sliced
1 clove garlic, crushed
500 mL (2 cups) tomato sauce
1 bay leaf
1 red pepper, finely chopped
pinch allspice
30 mL (2 tablespoons) cornstarch dissolved in
60 mL (4 tablespoons) water
125 mL (1/2 cup) sour cream

Method
— Preheat a browning dish at 100% for 7 minutes; add the oil and heat at 100% for 30 seconds.
— Brown the chicken pieces in the hot oil to give them an attractive golden appearance.
— Add the onion, garlic, tomato sauce, bay leaf, red pepper and allspice; cover and cook at 100% for 3 minutes.
— Stir, cover, and continue to cook at 70% for 12 to 15 minutes, or until the chicken is tender, rearranging the chicken pieces halfway through the cooking time.
— Remove the chicken pieces from the dish and set aside.
— Add the dissolved cornstarch to the sauce and cook at 100% for 2 to 3 minutes, stirring every minute.
— Return the chicken to the dish, blend in the sour cream, and serve.

Preheat a browning dish, add the oil, and brown the chicken pieces.

Add the onion, garlic, tomato sauce, red pepper, and seasoning; cover and cook at 100% for 3 minutes. Stir and continue to cook as directed in the recipe.

MICROTIPS
With Regard to Salt...

It is customary to add salt to vegetables when you cook them. However, when cooking with the microwave oven, you must be careful because any salt sprinkled directly on the vegetables causes them to dehydrate. You may, if you wish, add salt to the water in which the vegetables are to be cooked although in fact, we do not recommend the use of salt in cooking vegetables.

Entertaining

Menu:
Fettuccine Alfredo
Vegetables with Vinaigrette
Dressing
Guinea Fowl with Raspberries
Mint Parfait

It might seem rather mundane to serve poultry when you entertain, but the menu we suggest here will change your mind on that score! Guinea fowl still ranks as an unusual choice of bird and it is one that will fill your guests with awe. This particular fowl was not domesticated until relatively recent times, and it retains a taste that is sufficiently reminiscent of wild game to set it apart from most poultry. Many good cooks therefore suggest that you complement its flavor with a sauce, glaze or stuffing made with acidic fruit. Although oranges and limes are obvious choices, we suggest a variation—raspberries.

Fettucine Alfredo is a dish so well known that it is a gourmet classic. The accompanying vegetables are also bound to be a success, even with the most demanding of guests: julienned carrots, tender mushrooms, and braised asparagus, chilled and served with a vinaigrette dressing.

To make your triumph complete, serve a mint parfait for dessert. The distinctive flavors of the ingredients make an intriguing combination. If you wish, you can round off the meal with strong espresso or brandy—and talk about the wonderful dinner!

From the Recipe to Your Table

You must plan your dinner preparation well if you don't want your evening of entertaining to become a worrying chore. Cooking a complete meal in the microwave oven requires the same planning as cooking in a conventional oven. Only the cooking and reheating times vary.

24 hours before the meal:
—Prepare the mint parfait.
3 hours before the meal:
—Cook the vegetables and prepare the vinaigrette.
2 hours before the meal:
—Prepare the fettuccine Alfredo.
1 hour and 15 minutes before the meal:
—Prepare the guinea fowl with raspberries.
10 minutes before the meal:
—Add the vinaigrette to the vegetables.
5 minutes before the meal:
—Reheat the fettuccine.

Fettucine Alfredo

Ingredients
1.5 L (6 cups) water
salt to taste
15 mL (1 tablespoon) oil
225 g (8 oz) fettucine
2 egg yolks
50 mL (1/4 cup) 35% cream
50 mL (1/4 cup) Parmesan
cheese, grated
60 mL (4 tablespoons) melted
butter
freshly ground pepper to
taste

Method
— Heat the water in a large
container at 100% for 10
to 12 minutes, or until it
boils; add a little salt and
the oil.
— Put the fettucine in the
boiling water and cook at
100% for 7 to 9 minutes,
stirring every 3 minutes.
— When the pasta is done,
rinse in cold water, drain,
and set aside.
— Blend the egg yolks with
the cream and add the
Parmesan cheese.
— Pour the melted butter
over the pasta and add the
cream and cheese sauce.
— Reheat at 50% for 3 to 4
minutes, stirring every
minute.
— Serve as an appetizer.

Garden Vegetables with Vinaigrette Dressing

Vegetables
Ingredients
1 bunch asparagus
4 carrots, cut julienne
225 g (8 oz) mushroom caps

Method
— Put the asparagus in a
dish with 50 mL (1/4 cup)
water, cover and cook at
100% for 4 to 5 minutes,
giving the dish a half-turn
after 3 minutes.
— When the asparagus is
done, allow it to cool.
— Put the carrots in a dish
with 75 mL (1/3 cup)
water, cover, and cook at
100% for 5 to 6 minutes,
stirring halfway through
the cooking time. Allow
to cool.
— Cover the mushrooms and
cook at 100% for 2
minutes. Let cool.

Vinaigrette Dressing
Ingredients
75 mL (1/3 cup) wine vinegar
250 mL (1 cup) oil
salt and pepper to taste
5 mL (1 teaspoon) Dijon
mustard
1 hard boiled egg, chopped
15 mL (1 tablespoon) fine
herbs

Method
— Combine all the
ingredients and mix well.
(The vinaigrette can be
prepared several hours
ahead of time.)
— Sprinkle the vinaigrette
over the vegetables 10
minutes before serving.

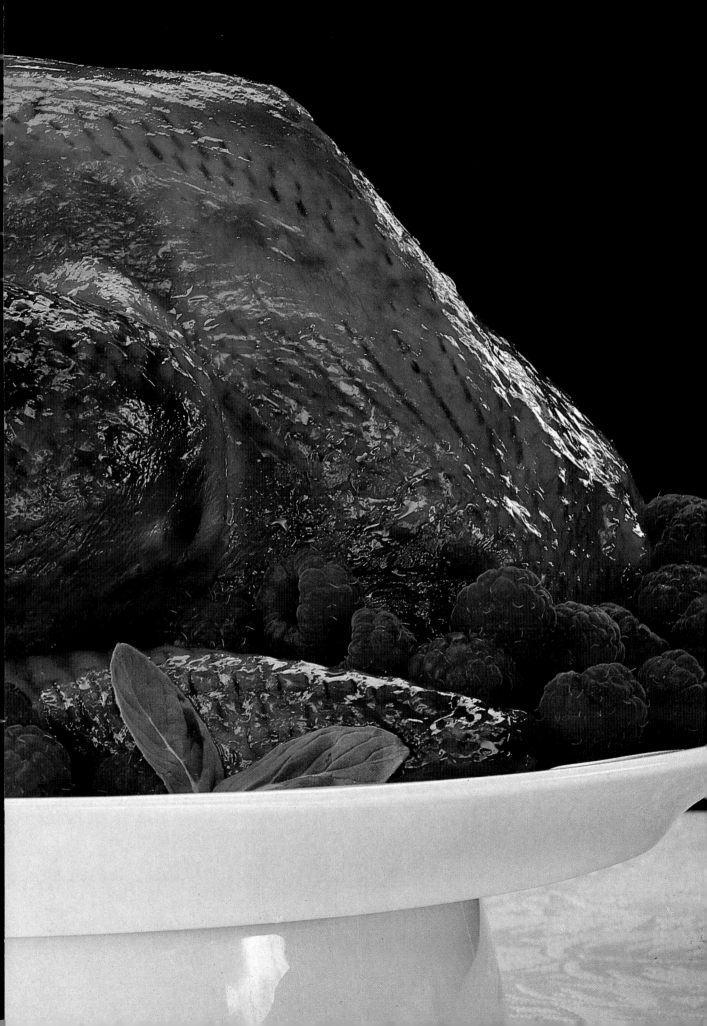

Guinea Fowl with Raspberries

The guinea fowl recipe offered here represents a fresh approach to poultry. There is an impressive repertoire of classic recipes for this bird, some corresponding to recipes used with other types of poultry that are considered classic. Examples include Guinea Fowl Casserole, Guinea Fowl Creole, Guinea Fowl with Orange, and Guinea Fowl Supreme.

Ingredients
2 guinea fowl
60 mL (4 tablespoons) butter, softened
60 mL (4 tablespoons) raspberry vinegar
30 mL (2 tablespoons) chicken powder concentrate
15 mL (1 tablespoon) paprika
250 mL (1 cup) chicken stock
15 mL (1 tablespoon) butter
15 mL (1 tablespoon) flour
250 mL (1 cup) raspberries

Level of Difficulty	🍴
Preparation Time	15 min
Cost per Serving	$ $ $
Number of Servings	6
Nutritional Value	495 calories 48.8 g protein 27.2 g lipids
Food Exchanges	4 oz meat 1 fruit exchanges 2-1/2 fat exchanges
Cooking Time	66 min
Standing Time	10 min
Power Level	100%, 70%
Write Your Cooking Time Here	

Method
— Combine the softened butter with the raspberry vinegar and pour this mixture into the cavities of the guinea fowl.
— Mix the chicken concentrate with the paprika and rub it over the guinea fowl.
— Place the birds on a rack, breast side up; leave uncovered and cook at 70% for 30 minutes.
— Turn the birds over and cook at 70% for another 30 minutes, or until the meat is tender.
— Remove the guinea fowl and cover them with aluminum foil, putting the shiny side next to the skin. Allow them to stand for 10 minutes.
— Meanwhile, deglaze the pan with the chicken stock, strain it, and skim it.
— Heat the 15 mL (1 tablespoon) buttter for 30 seconds at 100%; add the flour and mix well.
— Add the chicken stock to the roux, stirring well. Cook at 100% for 2 minutes, stir, and continue to cook at 100% for 1 to 2 minutes more, or until it thickens.
— Add the raspberries to the stock and cook at 100% for 1 to 2 minutes.
— Pour into a sauceboat and serve with the guinea fowl.

Mint Parfait

Ingredients

8 egg yolks, beaten
625 mL (2-1/2 cups) crème fraîche (available in specialty stores)
juice and zest of 1 lemon
1 slice lemon
50 mL (1/4 cup) crème de menthe
125 mL (1/2 cup) icing sugar, sifted

Method

— Combine the egg yolks and crème fraîche with the juice, zest, and slice of lemon in a dish.
— Cook at 70% for 5 to 7 minutes, without letting it come to the boil, and stir every minute until it becomes very thick.
— Pour the mixture into a bowl, add the crème de menthe, and cover tightly to exclude any air.
— Allow to stand for 30 minutes in a warm place so that the mixture thickens and the flavors are infused.
— When the cream mixture is lightly colored strain it, allow to cool, and add the icing sugar to taste. Mix well.
— Put into the freezer in an ice-cream maker until it is firm and smooth. Remove from the freezer about 30 to 60 minutes before serving.
— Serve in parfait glasses garnished with a sprig of mint.

Using Wines and Spirits

If you take the trouble to prepare a fine meal with poultry, you owe it to yourself to complement it at the table with the right wine. It is also worth remembering that wine and other spirits can be used in the cooking of poultry to enhance the special flavor of the meat. The following guidelines will help you choose the right wine for the very best results.

Using Wine in Cooking Poultry

As a general rule, poultry and accompanying white sauces are cooked with a dry white wine. A white bordeaux, for example, would be an excellent choice. You can use cider instead of white wine, as long as it is dry. However, if you are cooking game birds or poultry with a stronger flavor—perhaps because you have marinated it—you would do better to choose a robust red wine containing between 12.5% and 13.5% alcohol. Light wines are not strong enough for good results and vintage wines are rather wasted. Select an Italian, Algerian, or Spanish wine instead. You will find several on the market that have the right characteristics for cooking and that are reasonably priced.

Serving Wine with Poultry

It is usual to serve white wine with poultry. However, being a matter of taste, there is no reason why you can't break this rule, although you will likely find that a light wine goes well with delicately flavored poultry while a more robust wine suits game.

Using Spirits in Cooking Poultry

Madeira is a fortified wine that is used a great deal in cooking poultry, particularly domestic fowl. For example, Madeira may be added to the cooking juices from a chicken cooked with mushrooms; the result is slightly sweet, velvety sauce with a superb flavor. The alcohol evaporates in the cooking process. Another way to use spirits is to flambé individual poultry pieces in brandy, even if your recipe does not tell you to do so. Only a small amount of brandy is needed—the alcohol is burned off and the meat retains the subtle flavor of the brandy.

Poultry Terminology

Breast bone: The ridge of bone distinguishable on the front of all types of poultry. The breast meat is attached to this bone.

Capon: A rooster that is castrated so as to produce better meat for the table. An adult capon has been fattened and weighs more than a normal chicken. It has meat that is very tender, similar to a much younger bird. The ancient Greeks raised capons.

Crépinette: The name given to a variety of ground meat patties that are wrapped in caul—part of the stomach membrane of butchered animals, usually the pig. The ingredients include liver, poultry meat, etc.

Croquettes: Small round or oval patties usually made with chopped or minced cooked meat, fish or poultry, vegetables and seasoning. They are crumb coated and baked or deep fat fried.

Deglaze: To pour a liquid such as vinegar, a good dry white wine, cream, or spirits into the pan that has been used for cooking poultry or meat. The liquid is boiled and stirred vigorously so as to make use of the cooking juices, which become the base of a number of sauces.

Duckling: A duck less than two months old. Duckling is so tender that it can be roasted without any kind of stuffing or accompaniment.

Escallop: A thin slice of boneless meat (in poultry, usually cut from the breast of turkey) that is usually crumb coated.

Fattened pullet: A traditional method of fattening chickens was to raise them in a cage in dim light. This method stopped the bird from reaching full maturity and its meat was light and tender. The term "pullet" currently refers to chickens weighing more than 1.8 kg (4 lb).

Fond: A French cooking term referring to the cooking stock that is used for making sauce or for basting. A true *fond* is stock that has been made with the bones of meat, poultry or fish, aromatic herbs, and vegetables. A *fond blanc* (white stock) is made with uncooked ingredients and a *fond brun* (brown stock), with ingredients that are browned beforehand.

Fricassee: Meat or poultry cut into pieces, stewed and served with a thick gravy.

Galantine: A dish made from boned poultry, game, meat or fish. It is stuffed and rolled into a symmetrical shape and served hot or in aspic.

Giblets: Edible innards of a bird, including the liver, heart, gizzard and kidneys.

Gizzard: The third digestive pouch in poultry. It is used in stuffing or to make stock.

Glaze: "To coat" or "to baste" in order to give color and shine to poultry. In traditional Chinese cooking, duck is coated in a special glaze before it is roasted.

Jointing poultry: Cutting poultry into serving pieces.

Parson's nose: The tail of a bird at the base of the spine. The meat on the parson's nose is very fatty.

Poussin: A chicken that is slaughtered when it is between 50 and 70 days old. The meat is quite firm.

Quenelle: Quenelles are made from finely ground meat, poultry, game or fish and bound with fat, eggs, or cream. They are delicately seasoned, shaped into balls the size of an egg and poached in liquid.

Roux: A mixture of flour and butter that is cooked and used as a base for thickening sauces.

Stuffing: A mixture of finely chopped ingredients with seasoning used for poultry, vegetables, etc.

Supreme: This word is used to describe a boned and skinned breast of chicken, usually lightly sautéed or poached.

Tabasco: A Mexican sauce made with macerated hot red peppers, salt and vinegar.

Truss: To secure a bird with string before cooking it so that it does not lose its shape.

Velouté: A white sauce made from roux and white veal or chicken stock. It is used as the base for a number of related sauces.

Conversion Chart

Conversion Chart for the Main Measures Used in Cooking

Volume
1 teaspoon . . . . 5 mL
1 tablespoon . . . . 15 mL

1 quart (4 cups) . . . . 1 litre
1 pint (2 cups) . . . . 500 mL
1/2 cup . . . . 125 mL
1/4 cup . . . . 50 mL

Weight
2.2 lb . . . . 1 kg (1000 g)
1.1 lb . . . . 500 g
0.5 lb . . . . 225 g
0.25 lb . . . . 115 g

1 oz . . . . 30 g

Metric Equivalents for Cooking Temperatures

49°C . . . . 120°F	120°C . . . . 250°F
54°C . . . . 130°F	135°C . . . . 275°F
60°C . . . . 140°F	150°C . . . . 300°F
66°C . . . . 150°F	160°C . . . . 325°F
71°C . . . . 160°F	180°C . . . . 350°F
77°C . . . . 170°F	190°C . . . . 375°F
82°C . . . . 180°F	200°C . . . . 400°F
93°C . . . . 200°F	220°C . . . . 425°F
107°C . . . . 225°F	230°C . . . . 450°F

Readers will note that, in the recipes, we give 250 mL as the equivalent for 1 cup and 450 g as the equivalent for 1 lb and that fractions of these measurements are even less mathematically accurate. The reason for this is that mathematically accurate conversions are just not practical in cooking. Your kitchen scales are simply not accurate enough to weigh 454 g—the true equivalent of 1 lb—and it would be a waste of time to try. The conversions given in this series, therefore, necessarily represent approximate equivalents, but they will still give excellent results in the kitchen. No problems should be encountered if you adhere to either metric or imperial measurements throughout a recipe.

Index

MICROTIPS